FAST TRACK

FAST TRACK
A Handbook for High-flyers

Terry Farnsworth

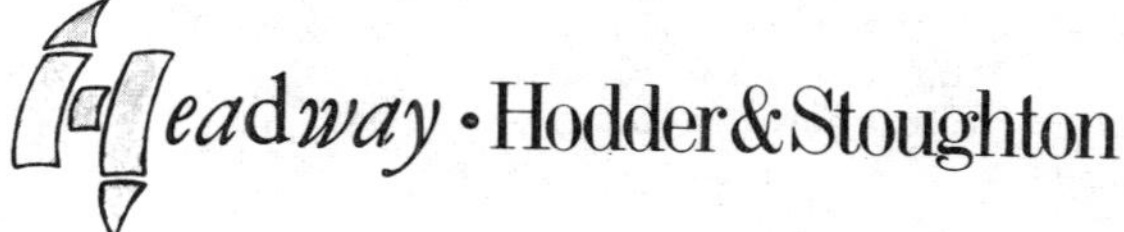

For all those Get-up-and-Go People who deserve to succeed.

British Library Cataloguing in Publication Data
Farnsworth, Terry
Fast track.
1. Business firms. Executive. Success
I. Title
658.409

ISBN 0 340 53462 1

First published 1990

Phototypeset by Input Typesetting Ltd, London
Printed in Great Britain for the educational publishing division of Hodder and Stoughton Ltd, Mill Road, Dunton Green, Sevenoaks, Kent by Richard Clay Ltd, Bungay, Suffolk.

— Contents —

Foreword xiii

Preface xiv

PART I : PERSONALITY IS THE KEY 1

1 Selecting the right company 3

Make sure the culture is right for you – if your face doesn't fit, you'll be wasting your time.

What kind of company are you looking for? How much commitment are you prepared to give? What kind of educational background is most relevant to different companies? Types of organisation: multinationals; family concerns; public sector; high-tech; retail; banks, building societies, insurance companies.

2 Getting off to a flying start 11

Tread warily for the first six months – it takes time to locate those hidden minefields.

Personal appearance: do's and don'ts. How should you furnish your office? Entertaining your colleagues: avoiding the pitfalls. 'Culture': should you let it show? Keeping fit: jogging, squash, golf, etc. Increasing your visibility. Being approachable. 'Walking the job'.

3 Winning friends and influencing people 19

Keep your ego in check – being *liked* and *remembered* is what really counts.

Company types who can help you: high flyers, old hands, experts, gossips, personnel managers, company 'characters'.

Using outside contacts for internal image-building. Watching out for 'dark horses'. Becoming a VIP's protégé. The secretary as confidant/intelligence-gatherer. Joining the right clubs (business, social, sporting).

4 Building a company power base 27

Inspire trust – it draws people to you like moths to a flame.

Building a network. Being excellent at your job. Being a good 'company' man. Cultivating the social graces. Charm. Being accessible: giving and receiving confidences. Keeping secrets. Doing favours, and knowing when to call them in. Being consistent – and flexible.

5 Staying sharp 35

Never be too busy to improve your skills – untrained troops don't win battles.

Developing a success strategy. Being your own toughest critic. Re-thinking your job. The role of formal courses. Planned reading programmes. Learning from your boss, peers, subordinates. Projects and special assignments. Job rotation: plusses and pitfalls. Delegation. Creating 'thinking time'. Testing your teaching skills.

PART II : PEOPLE ARE THE CHALLENGE 45

6 Coping with jealousy 47

Always try to roll with the punches – today's enemy could be tomorrow's friend.

Defusing jealousy from boss or colleagues. Making deliberate (but minor) mistakes. Letting others take the credit for (minor) accomplishments. Being your boss' eyes and ears. Socialising: pubs, clubs, restaurants. Entertaining at home. Being sensitive to others' feelings. Avoiding taboo subjects.

Developing positive attitudes. How to prepare effectively. Defining the audience's needs. Establishing objectives. Brainstorming for ideas. Developing a plan. What kind of notes? Using visual aids. Is it worth rehearsing? Dealing with awkward questions. Effective speaking and leadership: the importance of practice.

PART III : POLITICS IS THE TEST 87

11 Avoiding those killer mistakes 89

Never violate the organisation's unwritten rules – or you'll remain forever an outcast from the tribe.

Trespassing on others' 'turf'. Office affairs. Going over the boss' head. Being too 'pushy'. Name-dropping. Sarcasm. Boasting. Humiliating one's boss or colleagues. Flaunting other sources of income. Crawling. Misguided humour, lapses of taste.

12 Dealing with office politicians 99

Some business games can be lethal – either play to win or don't get involved.

Backstabbing. Rumour-mongering. Being kept in the dark. False promises. Spurious assignments. Fake promotions. Coping with a jealous boss. Resisting attempts to break your spirit with mindless chores. Vague objectives, inadequate authority, incomplete briefings. Dealing with attempts to sabotage your best ideas.

13 Negotiating useful alliances 107

Learn to make trade-offs – if you have something to sell, someone may want to buy.

The shifting nature of business relationships: 'nothing is forever'. Temporary alliances. Lobbying for support. 'Omerta':

the code of silence. Making profitable trade-offs. When it is prudent to sit on the fence. Avoiding 'fixers'. The importance of being flexible.

14 Keeping your career moving forward 115

Never rely upon 'career developers' – real high flyers manage their own careers.

Being opportunistic. Seeking greater visibility through company-wide assignments. Using training courses to make a favourable impression. Strategic socialising. Presentations at conferences. Building an outside reputation. Broadening your scope. Improving your qualifications. Developing subordinates to increase your promotability.

15 Profiting from panics 123

Welcome a crisis – there's no better opportunity for you to prove your worth.

Watching out for tell-tale signs of an impending crisis. Keeping calm: 'battening down the hatches'. The importance of good information: using your internal contacts. Running a tight ship. Taking stock of your staff. Pushing new ideas, especially money-making/money-saving ideas. Handling VIP visitors. Dealing with the media.

16 Impressing top people 131

Do what the expert yachtsman does – trim your sails to the prevailing wind.

Aiming for excellence. The importance of good performance, and of making sure it is well-publicised. Getting involved in company social events: societies, clubs, outings. Writing for company publications. Winning company awards. Cosseting the customer. Fostering good community relations. Being a good company ambassador: speaking at conferences. Avoiding 'ego-trips': putting the company first.

20 Staying on top 169

Keep on learning – an obsolescent chief executive lives on borrowed time.

The 'bottom line': sustained profitable performance. The key: keeping close to customers (product, quality, service). Abolishing 'them' and 'us'. Encouraging and rewarding creative employees. Consultation, participation, benefits, working conditions. Gaining commitment through self-motivation. Setting a good example. Dealing with rumours. Establishing the right 'core values'. Being courageous – and consistent. The role of training and development. The use of advisers. Knowing when it's time to go.

— *Foreword* —

I have always contended that business schools, and therefore business books, can only play a minor role in the success of any commercial enterprise. They may provide the theory, but the really important ingredients are common sense and a will to succeed. This book provides a down-to-earth approach and is of value to everybody whose ambition to succeed in business is matched with real ability.

The last ten years has seen a revolution in social and business attitudes, and I believe that this revolution – which involves the constant challenging of existing beliefs and then acting on them, will continue. We belong to the 'Why Not?' generation, particularly in the business arena, and we can count ourselves fortunate that this is the way it's going to be in the future.

Alan Sugar
Chairman, Amstrad PLC

— Preface —

This book is for those potential chief executives for whom the urge to compete is like an addictive drug. It is for future top policy-makers and people with vision. It is for those who need subtlety and political ringcraft. In short, it is for people who want to make it to the top.

The book makes three assumptions. First, that you are well equipped with the basic success qualities of intelligence, initiative and drive. Second, that you are dedicated to updating your knowledge and skills. Third (and this is crucial) that you are willing to learn how to market your talents both inside and outside the organisation.

This book will show you how to operate effectively in the real-life business world of competing egos and interests, principles and prejudices, dreams and delusions. It cannot guarantee your success but it *will* make it harder – *much* harder – for you to fail.

Why waste time wondering what your next career step should be? Take charge of your future. Read this book.

Part I

Personality is the key

I have bought
Golden opinions from all sorts of people.

Shakespeare, Macbeth 1.vii.44

Chapter 1

SELECTING THE RIGHT COMPANY

Make sure the culture is right for you – if your face doesn't fit you'll be wasting your time.

If you want to make it to the top in modern business you cannot afford to join the wrong company, for time wasted can never be regained. After all, by the year 2000 most organisations will be run by dynamic 'Young Turks' of 35–40, and retirement at 50 will be an executive norm. Given a career span of scarcely three decades, tomorrow's top executives can no longer hope to enjoy the luxury of an error of judgement at the beginning of their careers. When the starting-pistol cracks they must forge ahead or be left behind in an overcrowded field.

But what kind of company is right for *you*, and how do you make such a crucial choice? Only by *knowing yourself*, your strengths and weaknesses, your needs and motivations, and knowing what makes different organisations tick. For what really matters is whether you can find an environment in which your talents can prosper and where your limitations will not be overly exposed.

Be honest with yourself. What kind of atmosphere do you find most congenial? Do you thrive upon pressure or dislike taking risks? Are you impatient of bureaucracy, contemptuous of 'paper pushers' and only really happy when you are doing something new? Are you a workaholic for whom work and play totally coincide or must your weekends be a kind of sanctuary where you pursue other interests which enrich your life? The more honestly and accurately that you can answer such questions the more likely it is that you will make the right choice. Here are some of the leading options.

— Titans —

If you ever had boyhood dreams of a career in the Foreign Legion or, as a young girl, longed to be an air hostess, then join a dynamic multinational and travel the world at company expense.

Here among the faceless legions of the multi-talented you will need not merely ability but political skills of the highest order. For to thrive in such a competitive arena you must become not a sparkling individualist (perish the thought!) but a supreme example of Transnational Man (or Woman): cautious, conformist and, above all, totally untainted by cultural racism. Thrice blessed are the bland for they shall be marked out for early promotion! It is the perceptive 'smart ass' whose face does not fit.

To join this band of dedicated professionals, it is necessary that you pay your educational dues, and increasingly this means having an MBA, gained, it must be emphasised, not at some crumbling urban polytechnic but at one of the prestigious business schools where even the professors have had some industrial experience. The reasons for such high educational profiles in multinational companies are two-fold. Firstly, many of them are virtually overrun by business academics who are either 'researching' their latest books or, more profitably, are shamelessly huckstering themselves as 'consultants'. And since both professors and executives share a common belief in the superiority of academic management theories over 'seat of the pants' entrepreneurial flair, the next step follows as surely as night follows day: the exclusion of those who lack the requisite business school background from any position which carries real influence. By such means do oligarchies perpetuate themselves.

The second reason for this intellectual elitism is that most multinationals are convinced that their only hope of surviving ungentlemanly competition from emerging nations is for them to pack a more lethal marketing punch, hence the vogue for so-called 'global strategic planning systems'. Whether such panaceas will succeed in prolonging the lives of these leviathans is open to question, but of one fact there can be no doubt: there is invariably an explosive increase in bureaucratic procedures with which – so it is thought – only a crack business school graduate can be expected to cope. After all, if you have spent a whole year of your life reading scores of 50-page Harvard case studies, a little extra paperwork is no big deal.

Minnows

Compared with the smooth sophistication of the well-heeled multinational, the atmosphere in many family-owned concerns is about as restful as an evening at a Spanish bullfight. Bawled instructions echoing down bleak corridors, pounding machinery, non-stop pop music in the works canteen, jangling telephones in every miniscule office; only the toughest psyches can hope to survive such a daily ordeal. This is no place for the subtleties of the business school analyst; here it is more relevant to have fought your way through some decaying inner-city school or to have spent a few years in the Army drilling recruits.

But there are compensations. Powerful ones. First, you will never be bored, for the chances are that you will find yourself doing a broad-based job with none of the specialist support which you would take for granted in a multinational. Second, provided that you keep on the right side of the family mafia, your promotion prospects can be excellent and your remuneration and benefits surprisingly good. Third – and not least – there are often significant 'quality of life' factors (at least in the more rural areas) which can to some extent offset the draining effect of the panics and crises which will be the staple diet of your working life. Access to beautiful countryside, country sports and pastimes, the sense of being part of a close-knit community (both at work and outside it);

satisfactions such as these are hard to find in a glass and concrete tower with panoramic views over some characterless 'New Town'.

You also benefit from the 'big fish in a small pond' syndrome. Whereas in a global company even the presence of a vice-president may not be sufficient to quell the chatter in a busy office, as a senior executive in a respected family business – a pillar of the golf club and the local Round Table – you will command instant attention not only in pubs, clubs and restaurants but also at fêtes, garden parties, whist drives, dinner parties and virtually every other type of social gathering. This is all balm to the ego, and can be relied upon to produce a sense of individual worth very different from the rampant insecurities of many big-company executives.

You must, of course, be prepared to put up with the occasional knuckle-whitening incident: the chairman's son, full of Etonian arrogance, who asks (none too politely) if you could find someone to polish his Porsche; the Lord Lieutenant's wife who, over the walnuts and wine at a charity dinner, wonders how you can possibly endure such a *boring* job; the irate mother of a malingering apprentice who rebukes you for speaking harshly to her loutish son. But these are mere pin-pricks, and if you are a tough-minded pragmatist with plenty of stamina, a family firm can be hard to beat.

Bazaars

These are those large department stores, chain stores, discount warehouses and supermarkets where it is often easier to pass through the eye of a needle than to catch the eye of a gossiping assistant. To survive in retail management you need many of the attributes of the successful yachtsman: the nous to sense when the wind (of fashion) is changing and the ability to ride out a sudden storm. You also need luck, for in few other areas of business are bad decisions followed by such speedy retribution.

It can also pay you to stay single until your career begins to take off, for during those first frenetic years you will find yourself constantly moving to different jobs in different stores in different towns, constantly under pressure and working the kind of hours that would have won the respect of a 19th century mill-owner. Those stories of sex-mad trainee store executives, leaping from bedroom to bedroom like characters in a Feydeau farce, evoke only wry smiles and hollow laughter from those who survive this weeding-out process. 'Yes', they will tell you, 'we *did* spend a lot of time in bed. Nursing colds or catching up on sleep.'

For budding novelists and writers of detective stories, a retailing career provides a veritable goldmine of material. Coping with disgruntled customers, dealing with shoplifters and crooked employees, discouraging romance in the stockroom, witnessing the tearful reunions of mothers with their wandering infants: such an ever-changing human kaleidoscope provides a rich emotional counterpoint to the harsher music of the cash register. Indeed there are few occupations, except for the law, where people's motivations are so starkly revealed, and where the irrational becomes the norm and reason the exception. If you have writing aspirations, keep a diary.

You will never feel entirely secure even – or perhaps most of all – when you attain a top executive post. In the steaming jungles of the retail sector there are always predators on the look-out for those weaker than themselves, and a year or two's poor trading results will often attract the attention of takeover specialists who, if successful, may not wish to retain your services. In short, it is a world in which principles and ethics run a very poor second to the realities of the balance sheet. No wonder that 'company loyalty' is nowhere near as strong in retail companies as among those who work for industrial firms. One would hardly expect a turkey to trust the farmer.

Retailing is the ideal career for those who are easily bored and need plenty of challenge to keep the adrenalin flowing. There is no place for sentiment or for inflexible attitudes. You either strike it rich or lose your shirt.

— Fat Cats —

Banks, insurance companies and the larger building societies are the Fat Cats of the business world, the rocks upon which millions build their finances. Their recent attempts to project a more upbeat image have in no way compromised their essentially conservative role as reassuring symbols of probity and trust.

While working for a bank is now far more pleasant than in those not-so-distant days when hostile tellers peered at cringing customers from behind 'positions', most of which seemed to be permanently closed, it is still a relatively safe, well-ordered world, far removed from the bustling Bazaar or the rumbustious Minnow. Here the main qualities required for a successful career are caution, attention to detail and an ingrained suspicion of anyone applying for 'venture capital'.

You will also need to exercise considerable self-control, especially when studying a 'business plan' presented to you by some budding Edison, the success of which would require a higher miracle strike-rate than in a vintage year at Lourdes. Even in the more relaxed atmosphere of today's shrub-infested bank, it is still thought impolite to laugh in a customer's face.

When you arrive at the higher echelons of the Fat Cat world you will find yourself moving in the same mysterious circles as your slightly grander cousins in stockbroking and merchant banking. There is the same emphasis upon 'discretion' and 'gentleman's agreements', the same shunning of publicity and self-promotion. In short, this is no place for the bow-tied back-slapper or the kind of tasteless extrovert who tells risqué stories to visiting sheiks. You must be prepared to muzzle your individualism and to merge into the crowd. 'Soundness' is all. Let others play the fool.

— Futurists —

If you would be bored by labouring in overcrowded offices and seek a more unconventional environment, then join a company which is run by zealots, where the only thing that matters is your creativity. These are the Futurists: small, high-powered, highly technical organisations where the Board may be a bunch of young, bearded fanatics, dedicated to expanding the frontiers of knowledge and living to work rather than working to live.

Joining them may not be easy. You will need, as a minimum, a good honours degree in some relevant science and a few years' experience in either a research institution or a respected commercial laboratory. Above all, you will need to be an enthusiast, unencumbered by overly restrictive domestic ties or by distracting hobbies and sporting interests. If the job demands that you stay late several evenings a week or that you frequently work at weekends, so be it. You must give of your talents whenever they are required, not switch them off like a light after 'working hours'.

In return you will be free to concentrate upon your work without having to endure either the life-shortening crises of the Minnow or the savage in-fighting of the more ruthless Titans and Bazaars. There will be little bureaucracy to shackle your creativity, no job descriptions (you create your own) and no 'salary administration department' to ensure that your rewards do not exceed those of some long-serving mediocrity. Nor will you be expected to dress in accordance with some dreary formula which sees anything other than a white shirt or blouse and a business suit as a frontal attack upon western values. Jeans, slacks, see-through blouses, open-necked shirts, even a discreet medallion will be perfectly acceptable; indeed, they enhance the dedicated, high-powered scientist image which can so impress visiting dignitaries.

— Dodos —

To scale the commanding heights of a state-owned concern, you will need to blend the political talents of the Titaneer with the social skills of a senior Fat Catter. Gone are the days when you could expect to hide behind the skirts (or trousers) of government ministers when some horrendous gaffe had been exposed by the press. Today's top executive in a major Dodo must expect to stand upon his or her own feet.

This puts a premium upon communication skills, particularly the ability to be 'good on television' and to handle a press conference with confidence and flair. Again, in stark contrast to the old-style Dodo executive for whom the customer often seemed a tiresome distraction from political power-games, today's Dodo supremo must keep close to the customer or risk being thrown to the journalistic wolves. Such skills are not easily developed at the lower echelons of the typical public sector organisation and it is better to have spent a few years 'shooting the rapids' in advertising or public relations or in the marketing department of a thrusting Titan before moving to the calmer environment of a Dodo.

And you must be *patient*. Patient with penny-pinching civil servants. Patient with vote-catching politicians. Patient with government enquiries. Patient with professional dirt-diggers who may be more concerned with their own than with the public good. To succeed in a Dodo you need to be a stayer, not a resigner. You must see yourself as commanding an ocean liner which cannot be expected to outrun a speedboat. But when the speedboat has long since exhausted its fuel the liner will still sail serenely on. Working for a Dodo is a long-haul voyage, *not* a jolly afternoon at the rowing club.

One final point. If none of these options appeals to you, it may be that you are one of life's natural self-employed, destined to soar like an eagle above the toiling masses. But even if this is so, you should still carry on reading this book. After all, self-employment is a most hazardous business and you never know when you may be brought down to earth.

Chapter 2

GETTING OFF TO A FLYING START

Tread warily for the first six months – it takes time to locate those hidden minefields.

Joining a company is like getting married: the first six months is a voyage of discovery, of mutual exploration of each other's personality. It is a period when the stakes are high for it is then that the vital seed corn is sown that will determine the quality of the future harvest. It is a time when initial impressions are made that may linger on like labels that never seem to come unstuck.

Whatever your rank in the company hierarchy, whether you are a senior executive or a management trainee, you have one overwhelming need: to learn as much as possible about your new organisation and to master the essentials in the shortest possible time. But what are 'the essentials'? Certainly not the kind of unappetising stodge which is so frequently served up on company 'induction courses': banal history lessons about 'how it all began'; overblown details of products and services; and, not least, highly confusing organisation charts which leave a distinct impression of managerial over-manning. This is simply the sort of public relations pap which would be offered to any passing company visitor or used to impress gullible young graduates at recruitment interviews. It has nothing to do with what you *really* need to know: how to make a favourable impact and avoid transgressing the unwritten rules.

But how can you lock into your new company's values and speed up your acceptance as a well-adjusted employee? There are five key areas which require particular attention.

— Personal Appearance —

Unless you have fetched up on the wilder shores of advertising and public relations where colourful shirts and polka-dot bow ties may happily co-exist with outrageous minis, you would be well advised to dress conservatively and to wear the prevailing company uniform. For, despite the trend towards 'smart casual' (jeans, slacks, sweaters, etc.) at company social functions and sometimes even at courses and conferences, it is wiser to play it safe during office hours and to avoid anything which may smack of an unwelcome individualism. In most large organisations, men who wear charcoal grey suits, white shirts and innocuous ties are not merely proclaiming their membership of the executive club; they are also signalling that they possess other much-prized qualities of good taste and discretion. So eschew those 'sharp' Italian suits and keep old school ties for reunion dinners. Even in the City and the higher civil service, such tribal insignia are now regarded as 'divisive'. Let others discover your background for themselves.

'Smart yet unobtrusive' is a pretty sound guideline. For men, the rules are simple: better clean-shaven than a moustache, better a moustache than a beard and better a beard than undisciplined waves breaking over your collar. For women the list of prohibitions is rather more daunting: no coloured tights, no minis, no see-through blouses; no over-tight skirts, no 'provocative' necklines; no 'absurdly high' heels, no avant-garde hairstyles. And absolutely *no* 'inflammatory' fragrances. In short, unless you keep your sexuality under strict control, you risk being seen as a marauding Delilah, distracting vulnerable Samsons from their dedicated labours. Such are the fantasies of executive chauvinists who have yet to learn that women dress to please themselves.

Decorating your office

Even as a senior executive, your freedom to decorate your office to your personal taste may be severely constrained: there is usually a strictly-enforced company policy on such matters which may give you a limited choice of colours but little else. After all, organisations can scarcely be expected to encourage even greater displays of one-upmanship than those which currently exist between executives who are supposed to be working as a team.

Nevertheless, despite any restrictions governing furniture and fittings, there are still plenty of opportunities for self-expression. Here again let your watchword be 'inconspicuous good taste', for whatever you choose will be seen as reflecting your personality; visible evidence of qualities which may be hidden during the working week. Even people who have been colleagues for years often surprise each other with casual references to interests and accomplishments which none had suspected.

What you choose to put both *on* and *in* your bookcase can be extremely revealing. The 'company' man or woman will give pride of place to plaques or shields extolling their long years of service with the firm or to photographs of themselves shaking hands with the MD. Executives with a desire to impress the gullible will festoon the walls of their offices with framed certificates of their professional qualifications. Photographs of smiling spouses and of unusually grave-looking children will be the choice of those who wish to signal that they are solid, home-loving types who are beyond the reach of sexual predators, and can be relied upon to devote their energies to their work. For a newcomer to a company, such family mementos can be particularly appropriate, whereas diplomas and certificates may be seen as 'showing off'.

It is a mistake to cram your bookcase with erudite management textbooks, especially if most of them are in such mint condition that they generate suspicions that they have never been opened. A sprinkling of management classics is perfectly acceptable, but leaven them with a few good business biographies and pop psychologies which will convey the impression that you are a thinker and strategist, not simply a narrow specialist with limited horizons. And of course you must leave a little space for company policy manuals and for a few of those ornate folders which are sometimes handed out on executive training courses with your name embossed in gold lettering on the cover.

It is easy to go wrong with your choice of pictures (or, more likely, prints) and to create the impression that you are either a vulgar populist or an out-and-out poseur. Anything which is not strictly naturalistic runs the risk of raising a few eyebrows, though Monets and Van Goghs are now firmly established in boardrooms where once Sir Alfred Munnings reigned supreme. Better to steer a middle course with a couple of Canalettos and perhaps a John Piper. In manufacturing concerns, there is nothing to equal an L. S. Lowry: an artist as fitting as Elgar on the Last Night of the Proms.

— Entertaining —

If you want to find out what makes an organisation tick, make sure that you eat in the company canteen. It is not only alcohol that loosens tongues; even the simplest of meals with a few colleagues can provide an abundant harvest of information, ranging from wildcat rumours and slanderous gossip to informed speculation about imminent changes. But important though such gleanings can be, what you must really listen for are the underlying values and assumptions which are clearly taken for granted by your longer-serving colleagues. It is these which you must absorb as quickly as possible so that you strike the right note when arguing a case or when making a presentation at an important meeting.

Sometimes, of course, you may want to impress a particular executive or to discuss some delicate matter in the strictest confidence, in which case you need a more salubrious setting than the plate-pounding earthiness of the company restaurant. Nevertheless, it can be a mistake to bundle your colleague into your favourite bistro without giving a thought to any preferences which he or she may have regarding ambience or type of cuisine. Sometimes – particularly if you are trying to win support for a proposal – it can be more prudent to leave the choice of restaurant to your guest, for then he or she will be in familiar surroundings and hopefully more relaxed for listening to your ideas.

If you are considering whether to invite your colleague to dine at your club, think carefully before making your decision. Is there a reasonably friendly atmosphere in the club, or are strangers regarded as unwelcome intruders? Are there quiet places where business can be discussed, or are such conversations frowned upon and actively discouraged? Is the food reasonably palatable, or is it clearly derived from that forbidding, take-it-or-leave-it philosophy that has spawned countless atrocious school dinners? Are the club staff polite and helpful, or do they radiate a chilly hauteur?

One final point. Remember, if you are entertaining someone in order to learn more about the company culture, then you cannot expect to do so if you do all the talking. Your main role is to listen and to ask the kind of questions that will uncover that hidden agenda which gives every organisation its distinctive flavour. And by being a good listener you will acquire a reputation for wisdom and maturity that will be worth its weight in gold in the promotion stakes. Many a high flyer has talked his or her way into trouble, but few have ever given offence by listening.

Hobbies and interests

As a newcomer you are bound to be an object of curiosity as people strive to find out more about you, so that they can drop you into some convenient mental pigeon-hole. No one is going to probe too closely into your personal background, but hobbies and interests are quite another matter, since these are seen as legitimate topics for enabling people to discover what they have in common.

In the macho world of business, it is generally more acceptable to discuss sporting topics than cultural pursuits, which are sometimes associated with 'intellectual snobbery'. But even here there are pitfalls for the unwary newcomer, since not all sports are equally favoured. Golf, of course, is highly acceptable and so are rugby, squash, tennis and sailing. Hockey and cricket, however, are on the way down, while soccer is regarded as a pastime for hooligans. Among card games only bridge commands real respect, and you must *never* admit to a taste for poker (a game inextricably linked with chain-smoking salesmen). Swimming is OK so long as you belong to a club, but jogging is now in increasing disfavour following a spate of highly-publicised fatalities and injuries which have blackened its image with senior management. You should also avoid games like darts and ping-pong which are considered far too down-market for ambitious executives.

Cultural interests present even greater hazards than sports since some, like ballet, are regarded as 'effeminate' while others, such as twentieth-century music and painting, are thought to be dominated by 'poseurs' and 'pseuds'. However, if you are known to participate *actively* in a cultural pursuit, be it painting, chamber music or choral singing, then at least your interest will be regarded as 'genuine', since few people waste time on a hobby they dislike. Nevertheless, you would be wise not to trumpet your cultural interests too loudly, lest your colleagues (and superiors) should feel intellectually deprived. There is no point in generating gratuitous envy. Your talent alone will ensure plenty of that.

The one great exception to this 'low profile' policy is amateur dramatics, especially if you act rather than work behind the scenes. The reason is that such a highly extrovert activity is seen as wholly consistent with 'leading from the front': a much-prized quality in business leaders (though rather more rare than many would admit). Acting on stage, particularly in comedies, is regarded as evidence of 'unstuffiness', of someone who is prepared to 'have a go' and is not afraid of being laughed at. In short, the qualities of the amateur thespian are considered the same as those of the good 'team leader', part head prefect and part 'one of the boys'. You could scarcely wish for a more appropriate mix.

Being accessible – and visible

Different organisations have different expectations regarding how accessible their executives should be: to subordinates, to customers and, not least, to each other. While a few bureaucratic dinosaurs still cling to outdated notions of functional apartheid, with minimum contacts between departments, the vast majority champion 'effective communication' as the key to efficiency and high morale.

Increasingly, this means that executives who operate an 'open door' policy of making themselves accessible to casual visitors are greatly preferred to those whose doors remain shut, for without such 'dialogue' and 'personal interaction' good communication remains a pipedream. True, it may be annoying when some demotivated drone drops in for a chat while you are wrestling with a deskful of computer printouts, but a little forbearance can go a very long way. For it is precisely such gossips and rumour-mongers who can act as your eyes and ears throughout the organisation and give you plenty of warning about possible future shocks. Only the naïve put their faith in 'official' channels of communication: astute executives keep their ears to the ground. Above all, they master the art of appearing surprised when informed of decisions which they have known about for weeks.

Increasing your visibility means getting out of the office and 'walking the job'; going out of your way to introduce yourself to people you will be working with, especially those key personnel in other departments whose cooperation you will need to achieve your objectives. It is a mistake to put off meeting someone until you need his or her help with a problem, since it may well come at a time when both of you may be feeling upset. Dropping in at the company club or gym after work, arranging to have a regular Friday evening drink with a few colleagues, joining a company sports club, inviting someone to have a mid-morning coffee with you while you seek his or her reaction to a new idea; these are just a few of the ways by which you can make yourself a familiar figure around the company and build a reputation for sociability and *bonhomie*.

There are, of course, pitfalls. For example, a too aggressive approach to making yourself known can lead to your being labelled as 'pushy' or, worse still, 'brash'. And if you are seen as someone who is blatantly 'on the make' rather than as a genuinely friendly individual, then the barriers will go up and people may become distinctly tight-lipped. But there is no reason why this should happen provided that you remember the golden rule: talking may antagonise but listening *disarms*. The pen may indeed be mightier than the sword, but a quiet tongue can sometimes be more powerful than both.

Chapter 3

WINNING FRIENDS AND INFLUENCING PEOPLE

Keep your ego in check – being liked and remembered is what really counts.

It has now been more than six months since you joined your new company, and you have come through your apprenticeship with flying colours. By steadfastly avoiding controversy and by making yourself agreeable to large numbers of people, you are already beginning to win nods of approval and to be seen as a valuable future contributor. But even the most enjoyable honeymoon must come to an end. The time has arrived for you to show what you can do.

Like any good general, you must run a well-planned campaign or risk being rebuffed when you make your move. Before hurling yourself into a major project, bristling with changes which many may find unwelcome, it is wise to survey the surrounding terrain and note the location of any strategic features. This means identifying the people whose help you will need and going all-out to win their support. For these are the ones who can make all the difference between triumphant breakthrough and bloody defeat.

Virtually any interest which you have in common with an influential executive can be used as a gambit to win his or her support. This is where all that early socialising can yield rich dividends since you will almost certainly have acquired a wealth of information about the hobbies and interests of many of your colleagues: the perfect opening for a not-so-casual chat. You will need, of course, to be patient and diplomatic, since too crude an approach will almost certainly be resented. But nor need you 'pussy foot' around for too long. Most executives are accustomed to being lobbied and spend a good deal of time doing the same thing themselves.

— Patricians —

Every organisation has its elder statesmen, respected senior people with long years of service who are seen as the architects of the firm's success. Rich in experience and possessing enormous credibility, these greying veterans of a thousand campaigns are frequently not too far off retirement and are looking for an opportunity to make a last major contribution. What better way to end a distinguished career than to act as midwife to an exciting new strategy which could give the company a competitive edge? Especially if its author is a talented newcomer who might one day win through to the commanding heights.

If you can convince a Patrician that your idea has merit, you will have gained an advocate at the highest level who knows how to outsmart those company bureaucrats who might otherwise smother your brainchild with protocol. But beware, there is a price to pay for such heavyweight support: you *must* be willing to share the credit, and not seek to monopolise the spotlight's glare. And surely this is a fair exchange: a major success for a little harmless vanity? After all, to win the support of a company 'immortal' is a priceless asset. Like a Dead Sea swimmer, you will find it impossible to sink.

— High Flyers —

It may seem obvious to you to seek the support of other talented and ambitious people, but such a course is not without its perils.

The problem with many High Flyers is that their talents are overshadowed by their massive egos, thereby attracting a degree of dislike which sometimes spills over to their friends and cronies. There is also a danger that the more unscrupulous of the species may try to steal your idea and, with only the most superficial changes, pass it off as his or her own. Unhappily, talent and ethics are often uneasy bedfellows.

If, however, discreet enquiries reveal no such hazards, then try to get your quarry interested in your idea and stress that you will welcome constructive criticism. Any High Flyer worth his or her salt will leap at such a challenge, and the chances are that you will end up with a significantly improved proposal which will command the respect of even your toughest critics. It is here that you must display your own maturity by fully acknowledging the help which you have received, especially when you are making a formal presentation. To know that an idea has been 'critiqued' by a respected company 'brain' will favourably impress most senior management audiences. While it may not of itself be enough to win the race, it will at least get you off to a flying start.

— *Profs* —

Many good ideas founder because of their creators' inattention to detail, often relatively minor points which have been completely overlooked. Nevertheless, it is precisely such omissions which can provide a field day for the kind of nit-picking critic who, being devoid of creativity, resents it in others. Should you fall prey to this vulpine character you have only yourself to blame. Your headlines were good, but you forgot the small print.

Every organisation has its quota of Profs, quasi-academic people who are interested in knowledge and techniques rather than profit and loss or political power-play. Nothing pleases these specialists more than to be asked for their advice. Like butterflies displaying on a warm summer's day, they are only too willing to dazzle you with their expertise and to demonstrate how indispensable their services are. Tolerate their egotism, put up with their meanderings and you will find them more than willing to help. And make no mistake: their finishing touches to your master plan could prove vital in spiking your critics' guns.

— *Sunbeams* —

Some people become 'living legends' during their careers with their companies: sometimes, like Patricians, because of their accomplishments; more often as a result of their cheerful personalities which seem totally immune to even occasional 'off days'. Such Sunbeams are an asset to any organisation: in effect, they are walking anti-depressants who bring a touch of humour into humdrum lives.

It is no use looking to Sunbeams for the kind of help which you can get from High Flyers or Profs: analytical thinking is not their forte. Their value to you is not as critics, but as internal public relations officers who can powerfully influence what people think of you. A few favourable words from such well-loved characters and doors will open which would otherwise have closed. And what do you have to do to earn their friendship? Simply laugh at their jokes and show them respect. And never, never try to cap their stories. Yours is to listen, not to compete.

— *Godparents* —

Occasionally there are people outside the company whose friendship could be useful behind the scenes: senior executives of key customers and suppliers, prominent figures in the local community and those who are known to play golf with the chairman or to share an enthusiasm for weekend sailing.

But how do you meet such people and establish a mutually rewarding relationship? Sometimes it is simply a matter of chance: you sit next to someone at a business conference with whom you find you have much in common. Or you deal brilliantly with a major customer's problem and are invited to lunch with one of their top executives. But usually you meet them through some kind of club, occasionally political but more often sporting or social. It is generally not difficult to discover which clubs are worth joining. Find out how your chairman spends his or her weekends.

Needless to say, your contacts with Godparents must be extremely discreet; any crude requests for help in 'leaning on' your chairman are likely to be resented and lead to your relationship being swiftly terminated. You need the lightest possible touch: a quiet word while driving back from an evening's bridge at the club; a hint of a 'problem' over a drink in the bar. Then leave it at that and take no further action. To do so will simply label you as a tiresome nuisance and an excellent contact will be lost forever.

Insiders

Dotted around the organisational landscape, like early-warning radar devices, are the Insiders: people who always seem to know about impending changes long before they actually occur. Not to be confused with those incorrigible gossips who flit from office to office like indolent moths, Insiders are usually level-headed people whose confidence it is by no means easy to win. Sometimes, like personnel managers, they are naturally well-placed to know what is 'going on', but they can be found in just about any function which has a wealth of contacts throughout the whole organisation.

Gaining the confidence of an Insider can be worth its weight in gold. It is not so much that you are likely to be crudely 'tipped off' about some highly confidential policy change, for that would besmirch the Insider's own standards of professionalism. More likely you will be given a series of clues, tantalising snippets of information which you will be left to piece together for yourself. In a surprisingly short time you will become quite expert at 'reading between the lines' and of recognising the importance of apparently casual comments. But never be so crass as to thank your benefactor for saving you from making some horrendous gaffe. It is a game which he or she enjoys just as much as you, but one which is ruined by being openly acknowledged.

— *Referees* —

Every good salesperson knows the value of having an independent ally: a satisfied user of the product or service who is prepared to be contacted by a prospective customer and to corroborate the benefits which are claimed for it. Such 'third party referrals' are recognised as one of the surest ways of overcoming doubts about quality and reliability and of instilling confidence that the product 'works'.

If your idea has been successfully applied in other companies, a tactful approach to one of their senior executives could add a powerful new weapon to your persuasive armoury. Provided that the firm you choose is not a competitor, you could well acquire the kind of performance data which could sweep even the most doubting Thomases into your camp. And the more prestigious the firm in your particular industry, the greater the impact when you quote its experience. For despite all the cant about 'risk-taking' and innovation, most companies prefer to follow where others have led, thereby avoiding costly mistakes. Enlisting the aid of a credible Referee can stiffen the backbone of even the most cautious Board and assuage its fears of the new and unproven.

— *Confidants* —

The hand that rocks the cradle may or may not rule the world, but the one that controls an executive's diary is scarcely a force to be overlooked. Any sensible executive regards his or her secretary as a business partner, a Confidant who is privy to strategies and plans and whose help can be crucial to good time-management. An equally important secretarial function is that of grapevine-tapper and intelligence gatherer, and it is this which is sometimes inexplicably ignored.

But no role can be played without an adequate script, and it is vital that your secretary understands what kind of information could prove useful, and why. Having given such a briefing, you may be pleasantly surprised at the amount of valuable intelligence which begins to roll in. For example, your secretary may have heard that one of your most powerful allies (or foes) will not be able to attend your meeting, thereby enabling you, if necessary, to change the emphasis of your talk and to marshal your arguments in a different way. Similarly, if another executive's secretary has been complaining of having to stay late to type a lengthy report, then at least you know that you will be facing competition (and can do your damndest before the meeting to find out what it is).

Winning support for your first major initiative is a searching test of your fitness for the top, requiring a subtle combination of diplomacy and drive. In business, as in life, it is those who have the stamina to outlast their competitors who succeed in overcoming the toughest odds. And surely this is how it ought to be? Only the brave deserve a boardroom chair.

Chapter 4

BUILDING A COMPANY POWER BASE

Inspire trust – it draws people to you like moths to a flame.

Executives are like runners: there are short-term sprinters bent on immediate success and long-term stayers with a taste for strategy. Both are essential to a firm's survival and growth, but it is the stayers, not the sprinters, who win the glittering prizes. The reason for this is not hard to discover; sprinters win battles but stayers win wars.

To be a stayer, you need not only vision and talent, you need a company power base, a fortress from which to launch your campaigns. Like a medieval baron whose castle commands a view of the surrounding countryside, you can act without fear of being ambushed or of falling prey to a surprise attack. Even the occasional setback cannot permanently harm you. You simply retire to your lair to lick your wounds and – when the time is ripe – try again.

But how can you construct such an impressive citadel and what are the best materials to use? Should you try to do all the work yourself or should you enlist the help of others and be prepared to reciprocate when *they* need *you*? Are there any sure-fire recipes for lasting success or is it simply a matter of chance? And if the road winds uphill all the way will the rewards at the end be worth the effort?

Networks

There are some approaches to building a power base which, though once pre-eminent, no longer work. For example, whether you went to Eton and Balliol or to Roedean and Girton, you would be unwise to rely upon 'the old school tie' to spearhead your drive for company-wide influence. In an age when City dealing rooms resound with cockney accents, and whizz-kids from comprehensives represent Her Majesty abroad, trading upon one's background is considered extremely non-U, and even as evidence of a certain lack of self-confidence.

The most enduring kind of network is based not upon background but upon common interests and a willingness to give in order to receive. If you have the kind of job which interlocks with others, like a many-spoked wheel with your job at the hub, you have every opportunity to forge lasting alliances with those who need you just as much as you need them. There is an absurd tradition in business for certain functions to regard themselves as 'natural enemies': production and marketing, accounting and engineering (with virtually everyone detesting the personnel bureaucrats). Instead of tamely continuing such feuds, take the initiative in 'breaking the mould' by good communication and willing cooperation. For example, if you are a sales manager in the throes of negotiating an important contract, keep your production colleagues well informed of any special customer requirements, and win their backing right from the start. By building a reputation as an honest 'straight-shooter', you will be lighting a beacon which will be visible throughout the company. And in business, as in life, you tend to reap what you sow.

Nevertheless, however agreeable your relationship with a person, you should never take his or her support for granted. An idea which to you may seem quite brilliant may strike your colleague as extremely threatening. Here you must act quickly to defuse such opposition by making changes which will clearly show that you intend no harm to any vital interests. It is rarely profitable to risk endangering a network which can play such a crucial role in your ascent to the top. You cannot afford to be too inflexible. Those who compromise live to fight again.

Excellence

Being excellent at your job will not, of itself, win you a place in Valhalla, but at least it will get you nicely positioned at the gates. Professionalism, however, is not just a question of having the right skills: it is putting them to work so that *you* reap the benefit. Nothing will make your star shine more brightly than to gain a reputation not only for competence but also for keeping whatever promises you make. This is still sufficiently unusual in business for you to be regarded as some kind of saint.

Never turn down a request for help unless it is totally unavoidable; a satisfied colleague is a potential long-term ally whose support could one day be indispensable to your plans. And when your client is a *very* senior executive, it goes without saying that you should aim to produce the sort of performance that will get you talked about at the highest echelons. Even if it means taking work home at weekends and inflicting some minor inconvenience upon your family, do not flinch from doing what has to be done. They will soon forget that cancelled trip to the zoo when you celebrate your promotion with two weeks in Gstaad.

When presenting your proposal to someone who has asked for your help, don't hesitate to show off your expertise and to spice your explanations with liberal sprinklings of jargon. Doctors do this all the time in an effort to reassure their baffled patients that they are up to date with the latest techniques. And since some executives, like patients, are generally too embarrassed or too proud to reveal their ignorance, your professional competence is unlikely to be challenged. You simply assume that people know what you are talking about and refuse to be put off by the glazed look in their eyes.

— Doing favours —

Some of the most enduring relationships in business are the result of pure chance. You meet someone on your first day in the company with whom you strike up a lasting friendship or you attend a company course and find one or two kindred spirits over a drink in the bar. Whether it is personal chemistry or mutual interests which spark such friendships, they are always worth nurturing. They are, in effect, money in the bank, and you never know when you may need to cash a cheque.

Occasionally someone may ask a favour which, if you grant it, may cause you considerable inconvenience. For instance, you may be just about to go home after a particularly trying day when a colleague implores your help in dealing with a 'panic'. It is all too easy at such times to say 'no' or, worse still, to manufacture some deeply unconvincing excuse. But by cheerfully agreeing to help your colleague, you put yourself immediately in the position of a creditor. And one day you may want to call in your loan.

Nevertheless, in business, it is much better to be owed a favour than to owe one yourself, and you need be in no hurry to obtain your pound of flesh. The more that people have cause to think kindly of you, the more vigorous their response when you need their help. Never dissipate such goodwill with constant hints and reminders of what they owe you. Few will be found wanting when it comes to the crunch.

— Confidences —

The more popular you become, the more likely it is that people will begin to confide in you and to unburden themselves of their innermost thoughts. Stretched to the limited by demanding jobs, some executives are like walking time-bombs who crave the relief of a sympathetic ear or a tongue which they can rely upon not to wag. Little by little you find yourself becoming a kind of amateur psychiatrist whose job is to listen, not to prescribe. Even if you were to venture an opinion, it would be most unlikely to have any effect. It is not for your views that your friendship is valued, but for your ability to provide an uncritical audience, like a faithful spaniel at his master's feet.

Even the most self-disciplined executives occasionally feel the need to 'blow off steam' and to confide in people who can keep their mouths shut. The greater their confidence in your ability to keep quiet, the greater the flood of high-grade information on a bewildering range of company issues, some of which can be worth their weight in gold. Like a general standing on a strategic hill, you will have a bird's eye view of the company power game and can deploy your own forces to maximum effect. For while absolute secrecy must be your watchword, you can scarcely be expected to be totally unmoved. So by all means take action, but *don't* reveal your source.

Communication, of course, is a two-way street, and you must sometimes give as well as receive. As a giver of confidences, simply observe two basic rules: give as little as possible and proceed with caution. You should always aim to make a profit on the exchange, and you will certainly not do this if you are excessively generous. So don't give away too much too soon. Start with the pennies and work up to the pounds.

Charm

Charm is the lubricant which oils the wheels of a career, enabling you to glide from success to success. Contrary to popular belief, it has little to do with 'breeding' or with private education. It can be found in virtually every type of person, and has much more to do with empathy than with social class.

In practice, charm can cover everything from providing a shoulder to cry on to pleasing exhibitions of the key social graces: courtesy, sensitivity and natural good manners. It is *not* a weapon solely to be used against the opposite sex, a sexist delusion which has had its day. It is at its most potent in ordinary business situations when competitiveness and 'toughness' may be the norm. For example, suppose that you have given an important presentation and are asked a question by a rival male executive which shows that he has been half-asleep. Do you rip him to pieces with remorseless logic? Heap coals of sarcasm on his oafish head? Roll your eyes heavenwards and fume with indignation? If you are wise you will do none of these things. You will thank him for his question and answer it courteously. Let others give you credit for your saintly forbearance. You have no time to waste on such easy targets.

Meetings, indeed, provide boundless opportunities for displays of charm. As chairperson you can separate two warring executives with a timely quip which defuses tension and restores goodwill. Or you can encourage a timid member to contribute by not-so-subtle flattery or by protecting him or her against unwelcome interruptions. Above all, when you are presiding over an important conference at which all ranks are represented, you can win golden opinions by mixing freely with the most junior people present. Such displays of democracy tend to be widely noted and will lead to you being credited with 'the common touch'.

Never underestimate the power of charm: it can be one of the bulwarks of your company power base. While it cannot be a substitute for executive talent, it can make all the difference when other things are equal. The essence of its appeal is neither an 'upper class' accent nor a command of etiquette: it is based, quite simply, upon a respect for human dignity. And few people these days will quarrel with that.

— *Patriotism* —

While 'my company right or wrong' may not be one of your more compelling motivations, it will certainly do no harm if you let it be thought that this is so. Indeed, some large companies – especially US multinationals – demand a degree of conformance to company beliefs and philosophies which would be more appropriate to a medieval monastery than to the final decades of the twentieth century. The company is the sun around which your life must revolve; everything else must play second fiddle.

Be that as it may, even if you work in a more liberal atmosphere, you can still play the role of company patriot and wave the flag on appropriate occasions. While some executives shy away from company social events, there is much to be said for keeping a reasonably high profile and earning a reputation for being a 'good sport'. This means not just turning up at major jamborees such as the Annual Outing and the Christmas Dance. It also means volunteering your services for other key events such as Sports Day and the Annual Dinner for Retired Employees. There are always vacancies for people who are prepared to act as timekeepers for races or even as unofficial entertainers whose job it is to keep the old folk amused. Do not feel that such roles are beneath your dignity. Those letters of thanks to the chairman will make it well worthwhile.

Nevertheless, while becoming a popular figure has its obvious attractions, there are other paths to fame which, though less glamorous, can be just as effective. Becoming an office-holder in a trade association, giving talks about the company at local schools, arranging a factory tour for employees' families: these are only a few of the ways in which you can signal your corporate pride without appearing too egotistical. For it is vital to keep the spotlight trained on the company with you hovering modestly in the wings. Like all good politicians, you *can* have it both ways, serving the cause and serving yourself. All it takes is practice and a little self-discipline.

Consistency

What people fear is not having a tough boss, but a boss whose behaviour they find it hard to predict. Even a bully is more tolerable if he is predictable, whereas the boss who first blows hot then cold is a misery to all who work for him.

Projecting a consistent public image is a powerful way of winning support, since people will rejoice that you are 'always the same'. The question arises: what kind of consistency is most highly rated, both by your boss and those who work for you? From the boss' point of view the answer is easy: you should be conscientious, loyal and, above all, 'easy to manage'. In other words you should be the sort of person who can be relied upon to do what you are told without excessive debate and to endure occasional criticism without throwing a tantrum. Your subordinates, too, have similar 'humanistic' priorities with being appreciated for their work ranking as number one. In your dual role as both leader and follower you will go a long way if you observe these simple guidelines. There will be time to enjoy the luxury of being yourself when you have climbed to the topmost branch of the tree.

However, don't confuse consistency with inflexibility: convictions, like rules, sometimes need to be waived. There will be moments of crisis when you may need to scythe through normal consultative processes and act like a throwback to Attila the Hun. But provided that this happens only infrequently, your 'good guy' image will remain untarnished. People know that even enlightened bosses must sometimes take draconian measures. They will be more than willing to give you the benefit of the doubt.

Building a power base can be a laborious business but there is no alternative if you are aiming for the top. Without such a solid core of support, you will be a stranger wandering in a hostile wilderness, with neither map nor compass to guide you on your way. Strength respects strength in modern business and those who are vulnerable go to the wall. Remember: no one will hand you the keys of the kingdom if you look like a general who has never fought a war.

Chapter 5

STAYING SHARP

Never be too busy to improve your skills – untrained troops don't win battles.

Why do so many high flyers fail to fulfil their original promise? Some, undoubtedly, are over-rated, first blooming like orchids in a tropical storm, but then lacking stamina when the going gets rough. Others become complacent, convinced that they need do no more than tread water while waiting for the next gigantic wave which will carry them effortlessly to even greater success. Still more, appalled by the savagery of political in-fighting, trade in the spurs of executive ambition for the pipe and slippers of specialist jobs, far away from the sound of the guns.

But for every high flyer laid low by such factors, there are scores who simply run out of steam, whose creative juices begin to dry up. Like over-confident athletes who neglect to train properly, they gradually lose touch with the latest techniques, and begin to repeat the same old experience. Soon they find themselves struggling to keep up and start to lose their subordinates' respect. Thus, in a few short years, yesterday's superstars have become today's 'has beens' whose tomorrows look decidedly bleak.

Make no mistake: unless you stay sharp, this will happen to *you*; Change is a general who takes no prisoners. As new technologies rampage through business, scything down executive jobs, only those who have the foresight to keep on learning will deserve to survive, let alone make it to the top.

So what can you do to assure your future? Here are seven proven strategies for developing yourself which will give you an edge in the promotion race.

— 1 Re-think your job —

If you want to prove that you are ready for a bigger job, do the one you have *now* superbly well. This means not simply avoiding mistakes or even becoming a byword for efficiency. It means giving your job a completely new impetus through a lethal combination of creativity and drive.

Ignore your job description and go back to first principles. Ask yourself: why was this job created, what *purpose* was it designed to serve? Is this purpose still relevant or does it need re-thinking to meet tomorrow's challenges? What are the really crucial tasks, and how long will it take to make significant progress? The better your answers to such strategic questions, the greater your chances of making an impact. 'Play it safe' and you'll remain forever anonymous: take a risk and you'll stand out from the crowd.

Put every part of your job on trial for its life and discard any item which has no purpose. Like an overweight person you have to get rid of the flab before you can build up the muscle. Make a bonfire of all those trivial tasks and obsolete procedures which act as a brake upon your creativity. Replace them with specific, measurable objectives where success and failure are equally clear cut.

Above all, recognise that the *job* is where you learn most of your executive skills because this is where you spend most of your working life. Your abilities are forged in the daily struggle to achieve your goals (and to counteract various forms of human cussedness!). Don't expect to be motivated by someone else. If you want job satisfaction you have to motivate yourself.

Sadly, too many executives become complacent about their performance, feeling they need only 'coast' while waiting for promotion. The road to redundancy is paved with such delusions. There is *always* scope for adding value to the job.

2 Attend in-company management courses

Don't turn your nose up at in-house management courses; you could well be making a serious mistake. Not only can you practise some vital skills (effective speaking, listening, running meetings, etc.), you can also make valuable new contacts which may occasionally blossom into lasting friendships. Many a complex problem has been solved through the cameraderie of people who first met on a course and who shared some challenging learning experiences. The more demanding the course, the deeper the friendship: it can sometimes feel like having survived a war!

A particular advantage of in-company courses is that they give you an excellent opportunity to impress the training faculty. Despite those solemn assurances that there will be no post-course reports to superiors, the fact is that training staff are often asked informally about how certain individuals performed, and it is rare for such information to be withheld (even though there may be no formal written report). And since trainers are often a good deal more impressionable than those 'rational managers' they purport to admire, it follows that an enthusiastic, highly creative course member is going to win a whole sackful of 'brownie points' compared with the cynic or the delegate who rarely contributes.

Finally, when you are new to a company, there is no better way of absorbing the corporate culture than to attend a few 'induction courses'; not so much those rather mechanical recitals of company history and products as those which deal with general management issues. Whatever philosophies the trainers may be preaching, it is the subsequent discussion periods which can point up the differences between theory and practice. Listen with particular care to any contributions made by long-serving company speakers whose frankness can sometimes be extremely revealing. After all, the ability to distinguish between fact and fantasy can make all the difference between whether you succeed or stagnate.

To summarise: in-company courses can generate new contacts; help you to make your mark; and deepen your understanding of the 'company culture'. Never be 'too busy' to attend such meetings. They are an investment in your future success.

— 3 Keep up your reading —

Reading management books won't make you an outstanding manager, but not to read at all is to dice with redundancy. In today's fast-moving business world, past triumphs mean very little, since they were victories gained on yesterday's problems. It is *tomorrow's* challenges that really count.

Don't waste your time on books which merely churn up the same old ground; instead, keep alert for those which signal the shape of things to come. Some books which only a decade ago seemed highly futuristic – for example, Alvin Toffler's *The Third Wave* – now appear both realistic and practical. The lesson for ambitious executives is clear: draw up a list of top-flight business journals and read the book review pages extremely carefully. Make a note of any titles which seem to be breaking new ground, and either order them through the company library or invest in them yourself. Rest assured: you will not become bankrupt. The number of books with something new to say will be relatively small: you will be lucky to find more than a dozen a year.

Keeping a notebook can help you to capture a book's key ideas; a few main headings are usually all that is required. Another useful technique is to read a chapter and then challenge yourself to remember just two or three important points (if you fail the test, then re-read the chapter). As you become more skilled at extracting the essence of a book or article you will find that your appetite for reading increases. What was formerly a chore now becomes a pleasure, a welcome result of such 'effective reading' techniques.

Ignore any troglodyte senior managers who boast that they've never read a book on management in their lives; often their performance makes this only too clear. Just as lawyers and architects cannot hope to remain in business unless they keep abreast of the latest developments, so no professional executive buries his or her head in the sand. Make no mistake: the price of survival is continual self-improvement. Fall asleep and you may never wake up.

— 4 *Learn from the boss* —

If you're lucky enough to work for an outstanding boss, you have a wonderful opportunity to sharpen your performance; it's like attending a daily master-class. But to get the best of the relationship you need to follow a simple formula: observe, analyse, ask questions and practise.

Observe the kind of things your boss does which make him or her so effective. Watch how such persons manage their time; how they jot down those 'to do' lists at the beginning of each day; the way they lobby for support before an important meeting; how they adapt their approach to different personalities. *Analyse* what you have observed and reflect on why they acted the way they did. If there is anything you don't understand, then *ask them to explain*; you'll find them more than willing to share their expertise. After all, the better you perform, the fewer problems for them. And to have a first-class successor waiting in the wings gives a definite boost to their own promotion prospects.

Practise what you have learned, and if something doesn't work, then ask more questions until you are sure just why it went wrong. Above all, welcome (indeed insist upon) the frankest possible criticism; to get the best from the relationship there should be no pulled punches. The key question to ask is always 'why?' (not 'how?'), for this unlocks the secrets of both strategy and timing, and enables you to see how the pieces fit together. And the higher you climb on the executive ladder, the more you will need to think strategically, not simply react to a competitor's moves.

For good or ill, the immediate boss in any situation exerts a potent influence on the working group. He or she sets objectives, provides leadership, appraises performance and allocates rewards. In effect, the boss is 'the company', a living example of management practice who can enrich or impoverish people's working lives. So if you report to a 'winner', you're in a privileged position, since you are learning your trade from an acknowledged master. Make the most of your opportunity while it lasts. Such persons are always in short supply.

5 Learn from colleagues – and subordinates

However talented you may be, never be too proud to learn from able competitors: to be stiff-necked is to risk losing the race. If a colleague has a talent which you wish you possessed, don't waste time on pointless envy; either do your best to pick his or her brains, or discuss with your boss how to get some formal training. What you should *never* do is to try to convince yourself that the skill that you lack doesn't really matter; this is simply to offer a hostage to fortune. Having identified a gap in your promotion armoury, make filling it a prime self-improvement objective.

Similarly, use your subordinates as a learning resource. For example, if you need some help at making presentations or chairing meetings, ask your people to critique your performance and help you to pinpoint any major weaknesses. Encourage them to speak frankly, and don't get upset if they take you at your word. To learn from mistakes is the mark of a leader, and if you can get your subordinates to give you some honest feedback, you'll find it much easier to correct your faults.

Remember: the livelier and more creative the people who work for you, the greater the benefit to your own development, since it means that you will constantly be kept on your toes. Encouraging them to come up with new ideas and to challenge yours is an excellent way of increasing group productivity, as well as of having a great deal of fun. Good subordinates keep you sharp: dull ones can make you dangerously complacent.

6 Seek out projects and special assignments

Sometimes a company may be keen to investigate a new method or system but wants to do so in a way that minimises risk. The classic response to this dilemma is to set up a 'task force' to handle the project whose members may be drawn from a wide range of functions. Never turn down opportunities to join such teams. They give you a chance to break new ground and to work with some of the firm's most talented people.

There is nothing to equal the excitement of a major project which brings you into contact with a variety of disciplines, and enables you to appreciate what each can contribute. New knowledge, new skills, new contacts: such a project can be a dynamic learning event which compresses many years of business experience into a few short months or even weeks. Not surprisingly, to be selected for a task force is often a sign that you are on your way up, and your performance is likely to be closely watched. Two factors in particular will come under scrutiny: your ability to apply your specialist knowledge and your willingness to work as a member of a team. In the demanding environment of an important project, with tight deadlines and often limited resources, both qualities are likely to be tested to the full.

Nevertheless, for every glamorous company-wide assignment there are many more relative 'mini projects' which can also provide you with valuable experience and give you a chance to practise new skills. Many of these smaller-scale investigations are designed to solve specific problems encountered by a particular function or department. While some may involve two or three people working together, others are simply 'one-man bands': individuals who have been assigned to study a problem and to come up with proposals for an effective solution. Again, such 'troubleshooting' activities can offer excellent opportunities, not only to enrich your experience but also to test your powers of persuasion. Having to sell a new method to people who may be highly resistant to change is no mean challenge to any ambitious executive. Indeed, you can scarcely have too much practice.

'Mini projects' almost always depend upon the boss' willingness to delegate, since they may well be related to certain long-standing problems: 'skeletons in the cupboard' which have never been properly tackled. Encourage your boss to delegate by pointing out the benefits to him or her: more time to deal with bigger problems and more time to work on new ideas. Most bosses will find this an attractive proposition.

— 7 *Test your teaching skills* —

No one learns more about a subject than those who are required to teach it to others, especially if they are expected to defend their views in open debate. As the costs of external management courses continue to escalate, more and more companies are using their own executives on in-house management courses, particularly in areas such as marketing and finance.

If you are invited to contribute to such a programme, agree at once: it will provide you with three superb self-development opportunities. First, to practise your personal communication skills; second, to project an authoritative image of both yourself and your function; and third, to harvest a new idea on a problem which may be troubling you, suggested perhaps by a member of the course. These are all major benefits which will handsomely repay the investment of your time.

Don't refuse on the grounds that you're 'no good' at public speaking: arrange to get some training! Even if your company doesn't run its own effective speaking courses, there are plenty of short and relatively inexpensive outside seminars which can quickly bring you up to a reasonable standard. After all, you don't have to be a fireball platform orator to function effectively on an in-company course. You simply need to apply a few basic techniques and take care to avoid some of the more glaring pitfalls.

One final point. If you want to stay sharp, learn to manage your own development: don't abdicate responsibility to the training department. Many research studies have shown that what people learn for themselves, through their own self-motivation, makes a far greater impact than anything which reaches them second hand. The lesson is clear: whether you continue to grow depends upon how willing you are to keep on challenging yourself. *Welcome such challenges*. To shun them is to jeopardise your future career.

Part II

People are the challenge

Cheer up, the worst is yet to come.

Philander Chase Johnson, Shooting Stars

Chapter 6

COPING WITH JEALOUSY

Always try to roll with the punches – today's enemy could be tomorrow's friend.

During the past decade, one of the most successful products of the management development industry has been 'teambuilding' or, more latterly, 'teamworking'. Like some gigantic tidal wave pounding the sea walls of managerial inertia, the 'let's all work together' movement has engulfed virtually everything in its path, including, sometimes, common sense.

For unpalatable though it may be to idealists, the fact is that being an executive in today's combative business climate is a hazardous, high-risk and, above all, intensely *competitive* occupation. Teamworking, admittedly, can generate many powerful benefits: a sense of common purpose, a better use of resources and, not least, a greater respect for others' contributions. But it can never cure that insatiable itch which spurs on any truly talented individual: the urge to shine, to excel, to beat the competition out of sight.

There are no rules in such a contest, and not every protagonist is prepared to fight fairly. The more gifted you are – the more that you stand out from the crowd – the more likely it is that you will become the object of envy and suspicion. And deeply though you may despise such feelings, you cannot afford to ignore them. You must learn how to defuse such lurking time-bombs or risk your career being blown off course. Here are some techniques which will help to protect you.

— Flattery —

Had Cinderella deigned to flatter her less attractive sisters, she would not only have been permitted to attend the ball, they would probably have offered her a lift in their coach. In the real business world where the talented few struggle to avoid being swamped by the mediocre many, there is nothing to equal the power of flattery. It is the lubricant which has oiled many a glittering career, and a potent antidote to most forms of jealousy.

Pared to its essentials, flattery is the art of reflecting a person's idealised self-image, of providing reassurance that his or her judgement is sound. Unless you are dealing with an out-and-out egomaniac (admittedly not a wholly uncommon occurrence), it is rarely wise to indulge in blatant falsehoods, since such crudities are all too easy to detect. Skilled flatterers do not tell lies: they simply exaggerate the truth. Thus if a somewhat obese boss has lost a few pounds in weight, the flatterer murmurs that he or she is 'looking quite trim'; a merely competent presentation is described as 'excellent', while a fairly obvious suggestion is hailed as 'highly perceptive'. For maximum effect, the flattery should be delivered, not in a fawning tone, but in a casual, throw-away manner that makes it sound completely natural and spontaneous. Brevity and credibility go hand-in-hand.

Flattering colleagues successfully – particularly those who may be in a position to block your ideas – calls for much greater subtlety. A highly effective gambit is to present yourself to your colleague as someone who is seeking the advice of an acknowledged 'company guru' on a particular subject (which indeed may be no more than the truth). Nevertheless, such an approach can be highly reinforcing to the person concerned since it provides independent confirmation of his or her self-image. And few people object to being told that they are right.

On your way to the top you will meet many people who need constant praise and reassurance. Even the most aggressive individuals can be 'tamed' by the occasional application of a little soothing ego-balm which calms their insecurities and vanquishes self-doubt.

— Camouflage —

To counter resentment caused by your talent, it can sometimes pay to appear less gifted than you are. After all, jealousy usually results from feelings of inferiority, coupled with a dread of being 'found out' and replaced. If you can make it seem that there is less to you than meets the eye, you have a good chance of exorcising this most persistent of demons. But take care; it is unlikely to give up without a fight, and is always alert to recapture lost ground.

Camouflaging your true ability is far from easy. It means, for example, keeping a close rein on your tongue and stifling back that devastating retort or razor-sharp judgement. It means making your boss feel that he is a born leader, even though his dithering may be legendary throughout the company. It means making your colleagues feel secure and comfortable in your presence, and convincing them that you are 'one of the crowd' rather than a 'crown prince'. Above all, it means not taking sides when departmental feuds break out, but keeping your own counsel and remaining friends with everyone.

There will be times, of course, when there will be no need to dissemble; indeed when it is vital that you appear in your true colours. For example, whenever you are called upon to make a presentation to top management, you should not hesitate to operate at full throttle: impressing them with your intellect, dazzling them with your charm and generally performing to Olympic standards. Opportunities such as these occur all too rarely and must be thoroughly exploited. It is with your boss and your colleagues that you need to exercise caution.

However, even after a major boardroom triumph, you can regain your 'credibility' with your colleagues by a judicious mixture of false modesty and self-denigration. Any latent envious stirrings will be quickly extinguished by such remarks as 'I was lucky to have had such an easy ride' or 'I wasn't too happy with some of my answers to their questions'. In no time at all you will be forgiven your success, which may simply be seen as 'a flash in the pan', an unexpected flowering of an average talent. But you will have made your mark where it really counts.

Making the occasional deliberate mistake (but *only* on relatively trivial matters) can also be a powerful method of combating jealousy, especially on the part of a boss who suspects that you are after his job. Nothing gives the mediocre nit-picker greater satisfaction than to expose the shortcomings of the infinitely more talented. It is all part of the 'there's life in the old dog yet' syndrome which causes aging millionaires to marry nubile starlets and burnt-out Lotharios to haunt hotel bars. But be careful not to over-use this technique, or it may suggest that you are becoming careless. Your reputation can tolerate the occasional smudge, but nothing so lethal as a real black mark.

Cover-ups

Everyone knows that contacts are important in business, especially those which are based on mutual self-interest. Occasionally, however, it can pay you to exhibit somewhat nobler virtues and to help cover up others' mistakes. Needless to say, such errors must be no more than mere trifles. A top-level investigation into a major debacle could place a question mark over your promotion prospects.

Nevertheless, helping your boss and colleagues to cover up minor mistakes can be a useful way of putting them in your debt and of ensuring their cooperation when you need their help. The boss, of course, is well placed to show appreciation through a favourable performance appraisal or a well above-average salary increase. Better still, he or she may champion your claims as a promotion candidate, or strongly recommend you for a prestigious new assignment. But your colleagues, too, have an important role to play. After all, most new ideas require the cooperation of other people if they are to have any chance of succeeding, and sometimes your colleagues' support can be vital. For despite all that business school emphasis upon rational analysis and objective decision-making, it is whether the innovator is liked *as a person* which often determines whether the idea is accepted.

Another form of philanthropy which can help to defuse jealousy is to allow others – especially your boss – to take the credit for some minor improvement which was really your brainchild. The more insecure your superior – the more he or she may be feeling superfluous – the more gratefully your sacrifice will be received. Indeed, in many cases it is doubtful whether you will truly be making any sacrifice at all. In the case of a boss whose career is clearly in terminal decline, most people are well capable of putting two and two together. The boss will be seen as a puppet with *you* pulling the strings.

Grapevining

As management pundits never tire of pointing out, information is power in modern business, and the sooner you receive it, the quicker you can act. To get wind of some vital new development before your promotion rivals is to be more than half-way to winning the race. But, once again, it can sometimes pay you to be more altruistic, especially when the information involved is scarcely more than minor-league gossip.

Nonetheless, to share even the crumbs from your table with information-hungry competitors is yet another useful way of disarming jealousy. By judiciously feeding them with morsels of information which invariably turn out to be true, you will enhance your standing enormously, and will soon be regarded as someone who has an unrivalled knowledge of what is 'going on' in the company. In return, many of your colleagues will begin to bring you items of news from their own networks and occasionally you may learn of something really important. It is this ability to tap the numerous grapevines which abound in any organisation that gives the gregarious high-flyer a distinct advantage over the talented lone wolf. The latter believes that ability alone is sufficient to make it to the top. The former acknowledges that he or she may need some help.

Sharing the fruits of your grapevine with your boss will tend to allay the suspicions of even the most paranoid superior. After all, it is difficult to go on hating someone who keeps feeding you with information which enables you to appear to be on top of your job: such people are worth their weight in gold. However, there is no reason why the benefits should flow only one way and, using whichever method of communication you feel is most appropriate, you should not hesitate to indicate to your boss that you expect to be rewarded. The size of your next pay increase will tell you whether the message has got through.

Socialising

Remember: to defuse jealousy, you must stress your 'normality' and conceal your cleverness: few people feel threatened by an 'average' person. One of the surest ways of gaining acceptance is to take part in all those minor rituals which are part of the culture of every office: the Friday lunchtime drink with 'the boys', the Christmas party, the occasional game of snooker at the social club. By indulging in such popular rituals, you will quickly divest yourself of any remaining suspicions that you see yourself as a 'superior' being. Needless to say, any visits to the opera, ballet or to avant-garde art exhibitions should remain unreported.

Much the same sort of populist criteria should apply to your selection of clubs and restaurants. For example, if you intend to invite your boss or a colleague to dine at your club, make sure that it is one where they will feel comfortable, i.e. one where there are plenty of other executives. Few experiences could be more damaging to your career than for your boss to be patronised by some over-mighty waiter who is only really happy when ministering to dukes. Nor will he or she be impressed if they are glared at or sniffed at by some of the regular club members who regard all newcomers as unwelcome interlopers.

Restaurants also need to be selected with care. Again, avoid those modish places with grossly-inflated prices which cater principally for City tycoons and showbiz millionaires. Shun, too, those which seem to begrudge providing food at all, judging by the miniscule portions which they invariably serve. Instead, play safe by finding a middle-of-the-road venue where you will be neither bankrupted nor starved. And check that your companion likes the type of cuisine on offer. It takes but a moment to avert a disaster.

Entertaining in your home can be a good idea provided that you or your partner is a reasonable cook and, more importantly, that he or she is a highly discreet individual who can be relied upon to keep any family skeletons locked firmly in their cupboards. If your office colleagues are your sole guests, then let them make the conversational running and adapt to their interests rather than the other way round. But if you invite other guests, take care that they are likely to be compatible. The safest approach is to invite another executive and his or her partner, even though this may limit the range of topics discussed. Three categories of guest should be avoided like the plague: out-of-work actors (show-offs), would-be politicians (boring) and recent first-time parents who find their offspring so intensely fascinating that they can scarcely talk of anything else.

— Taboos —

Most people are wary of discussing religion and politics with their colleagues at work, and many show restraint when commenting on sexual matters. But these are only the tip of the iceberg, and there are many other conversational hazards which can cause a relationship to cool. Sometimes even the most seemingly mature and well-balanced individual has a 'blind spot': a topic on which he or she finds it difficult to be rational, and which can result in wholly unexpected changes in behaviour.

Frequently you will hear about these taboo subjects – and the reasons for an individual's reactions – from a friend or colleague.

Thereafter, having been shown the location of the minefield, you are in a position to avoid it. But often you have to venture into the unknown without any kind of map, and it is then that things can start to go wrong. Especially in the early stages of a relationship, it is always prudent to think twice before making grandiose, generalised statements which may unwittingly give offence to a colleague and stir up feelings of jealousy where none existed before. For example, if you have enjoyed a long and happy marriage to one spouse, it can be hurtful to keep on talking about your good fortune to a colleague who has been divorced three times. Similarly, if you have a daughter who is academically brilliant, what to you may seem no more than legitimate pride in her achievements may strike a colleague with a mentally handicapped child as quite insufferable boasting. Like a motorist on a winding country lane, you should proceed with caution until you know someone really well. The secret is to show interest in the other person rather than to talk constantly about yourself. There is no surer way of keeping jealousy at bay.

Remember: talent attracts admirers, but it can also make enemies among the less talented. The only way to draw the fangs of a jealous colleague or boss is to calm their insecurities by keeping your ego in check. Until you have reached a commanding position in the company, you must learn how to work with those who may resent you. It takes confidence, guile and a good deal of practice. But if you want that prize you don't really have a choice.

Chapter 7

GETTING RID OF POOR PERFORMERS

Use a scalpel, not an axe, if you want to be loved.

There have always been a few occupations where being fired is accepted with the same kind of stoicism with which one would normally greet the onset of the common cold: annoying, perhaps, but by no means a tragedy. Public relations, advertising, selling insurance: such jobs are for those with failure-proof nerves and a bottomless belief in their persuasive powers.

In most business organisations, despite the shake-outs of the past decade, there is still a tradition of caring paternalism which acts as a brake upon those 'hirers and firers' who seem to relish the occasional blood-letting. Yet sometimes such kindness can go too far, and the company loses its competitive edge. Costs rise, profits tumble and takeover specialists begin to move in.

However great your ability, you will only be worthy of a top-flight leadership role when you have proved that you can deal with poor performers. Just as weeds may choke even the choicest blooms, so failure to remove the patently inadequate will stunt the growth of talented subordinates and encourage them to pursue their careers elsewhere. Nor need this process always be harsh or painful. There are plenty of ways of sugaring the pill.

What determines your success is whether you can overcome those feelings of guilt which, if unchecked, can cause you to waver while the employee's performance continues to plummet. Instead of vacillating, act – and act *quickly*. To delay is to abdicate your responsibility as a manager.

Intensive care

One of the surest ways of making a martyr out of a poor performer is to appear to be acting without sufficient evidence. All too often management's decisions are seen as unjust and arbitrary: a lightning bolt from out of a clear, blue sky with nothing to suggest an approaching storm. No wonder that morale begins to sag as people ask each other 'who goes next?'.

The way to avoid such debilitating speculation is to show that you have given the offender every possible chance to overcome his or her problems. The first and most vital step is to communicate your dissatisfaction to the person concerned, giving specific examples of the principle shortcomings and encouraging suggestions for remedial action. Once you have convinced the individual that you genuinely want him or her back on your team, you can work out a 'performance recovery plan' in which both of you commit to specific actions. The plan will have clear-cut, measurable objectives, and will spell out the various activities needed to achieve them, plus a date by which improvement must be clearly visible. Perhaps your most important role is to act as a coach to the individual, and to seize every opportunity to pass on some of your own expertise. Don't abdicate your responsibilities to the training department.

More often than not, the strategy will be successful and the patient will emerge from intensive care with renewed motivation to do a good job. But occasionally there will be an unhappy ending to the story: the plan will fail and the individual's problems will intensify. It is now time for you to consider other options.

Light duties

Assuming that the company can afford to continue to employ the sub-standard performer, it becomes a question of finding a suitable job: one that serves a useful purpose and yet is free from the pressures of 'the bottom line'. In the competitive environment of modern business, such jobs scarcely abound and should be reserved for those long-serving employees who have been good contributors in the past, and for whom early retirement would not yet be practicable.

The essence of a successful 'light duty' appointment is that it should use at least one of the individual's main strengths and, in addition, should capitalise upon his or her company knowledge. For example, an experienced sales manager, formerly successful but now suffering from 'burnout', might be re-assigned as a product trainer or to a supervisory role in customer service. Similarly, a plant superintendent, no longer able to cope with the rigours of shift work, might be appointed to a coordinating role in purchasing or distribution. So long as the new job requires the use of an acknowledged strength – something which he or she *enjoys* doing – there is every chance of success. But if it simply continues to highlight a weakness, then failure is certain.

One of the key tests of your leadership skills is whether you can succeed in 'selling' such a 'light duties' job, not merely to the individual concerned, but to the rest of the organisation. Many dethroned managers will resent any suggestion of 'charity', and every organisation contains a few mischief-makers who will be only too willing to spread rumours about further impending 'demotions' and 'redundancies'. The only way to counter such difficulties is to issue a carefully-worded announcement of the appointment which sets out clearly what the job is intended to achieve, why the person concerned was selected and, not least, how the business will benefit.

Secondments

Another way of re-assigning (and, hopefully, revitalising) a sub-standard performer is to arrange for him or her to be seconded to another organisation. 'Sub-standard', after all, is a purely relative term, and many a performance which is seen as barely average in a company where standards are high would be perceived as outstanding in a less sophisticated firm.

Finding a suitable job in an equally suitable firm is generally a task for the personnel manager, though you may well have some ideas of your own. Once again, provided that there is a good fit between the secondee's strengths and the job's demands, there is a better-than-evens chance that the 'transplant' will be successful. Remember, however, that there can sometimes be a yawning gap between the old and the new company cultures which can make the early stages of a secondment particularly stressful. For this reason it is vital that secondees are given a guarantee that they will be re-employed in their old firms when their secondments end (though not, of course, in their previous jobs).

Secondments, like any form of re-assignment, can be something of a gamble, but when successful they can be very rewarding. Not only is the individual often re-motivated by a new challenge and a new environment; sometimes he or she may be offered a permanent job by the temporary employer and may, as it were, 'live happily ever after'. Even if the offer of a job is not forth-coming, a good performance will have generated much goodwill for the parent company: an important factor when the firm concerned is a key customer or supplier.

Sabbaticals and special assignments

To organise a sabbatical for an unsatisfactory performer may at first sight appear to be a ludicrously inappropriate response to a performance problem, as indeed it can be if two vital conditions are not observed. First, you must be convinced that the individual's condition is merely temporary: that it is the result of boredom and lack of challenge, not lack of ability. Second, the sabbatical or special assignment must involve a rigorous, in-depth investigation into a significant company problem, culminating in a written report and a personal presentation to top management. In short, it is an approach which can only be justified in the case of a high-calibre individual who is going through a bad patch, but whose chances of recovery are considered to be extremely bright.

Given careful selection of both individual and project there is every prospect of success. For the more analytical type of person, a period of research at a university or college can sometimes rekindle both intellectual curiosity and the spirit of adventure. For others who enjoy meeting a wide range of people, a programme of visits to important customers and suppliers in both the public and private sectors can sharpen minds grown stale with too much routine. In large organisations, similar benefits can accrue from projects which involve visiting different locations and interviewing managers from a variety of functions.

Sabbaticals and special assignments are essentially extended periods of convalescence during which the 'patient' is challenged to show that his or her recovery is complete. When successful, the results can be spectacular with 'born-again' managers displaying the kind of zestful performance which you may have thought had gone for ever. When this happens, you will have every reason to feel pleased with the return on your investment of time and energy. If it doesn't, it may be time for a tougher approach.

Early retirement and redundancy

When it is clear that the individual is either unable or unwilling to benefit from any remedial measures, then early retirement or redundancy may be the only way out. Since this is an area where it is all too easy for a boss to appear harsh and unfeeling, you would do well to have a realistic strategy for easing the pain of separation. This is not merely a question of financial generosity:

it also means helping the individual to strike out boldly into what may seem a frightening new world in which loss of income and loss of status are only the most prominent amid a host of worries.

If the person concerned would find re-employment difficult because of his or her age – but would like to continue working – you (or your personnel manager) may be able to find a suitable post with a distributor or supplier. As with secondments, many redundant big-company executives have expertise which can be extremely valuable to small organisations, and the probable drop in salary may not be too serious a problem if he or she no longer has any major financial commitments. An alternative is to use a carefully-selected 'outplacement' agency, and to reimburse the individual for any fees charged. Yet another effective approach is to subsidise the employee's attendance at courses which offer training in writing job applications and projecting oneself at interviews. Generous time off to attend such interviews is another benefit which is greatly appreciated.

By being generous and humane in your treatment of redundant employees, you will avoid those twin hazards which can easily result from an insensitive approach: a reputation for ruthlessness and a drop in staff morale. It is by no means uncommon for a redundant person to be seen as a martyr, a kind of 'awful warning' to those who remain. Even highly competent people may begin to feel threatened and to worry about their long-term career prospects with the company. Those whose skills are in short supply may be the first to seek a safer berth.

Dirty tricks

Bullying or otherwise pressurising an unsatisfactory performer is most unlikely to be productive since it undermines the very factor upon which any improvement must be based: self-confidence. Take away a person's belief in his or her abilities and you forfeit any hope of improving their performance. It is far better to voice your concerns in a straightforward manner than to indulge in various kinds of 'dirty tricks', hoping to force the individual to resign. No one will be fooled by such Machiavellian manoeuvres.

Nevertheless, despite their horrendous effects upon morale and teamwork, some executives employ a whole repertoire of devious stratagems to get rid of people whom they regard as 'useless'. One of the milder techniques – known as 'mushroom management' – is simply to keep such individuals in the dark: removing their names from circulation lists, omitting to send them copies of memos and reports and 'forgetting' to invite them to important meetings. By freezing them out of their usual routines and by denying them the opportunity to participate in decision-making, they hope to cause such alarm and despondency that the letter of resignation becomes a mere formality.

Much more brutal, however, is the opposite of this relatively passive approach: the relentless pressuring of the targeted executive with a veritable blizzard of new assignments, *in addition* to his or her normal duties. Required to produce lengthy reports on every new project and constantly badgered by telephone requests for 'progress updates', such individuals are gradually worn down until they either resign or ask for a transfer.

Only very popular, long-serving employees, or those with friends in high places are likely to qualify for somewhat gentler treatment. Such people are often assigned to evaluate external training programmes, or to attend conferences, and spend their lives in four-star hotels, dutifully asking the same two or three questions and writing reports which no one reads. Often such outcasts are channelled into some notorious company backwater, having been given a title such as 'internal consultant' or 'group adviser'. The fact that they are rarely consulted or asked for their advice is, for them, irrelevant. What matters is that the company has recognised their experience and 'statesmanship'.

Sudden death

In business, as in life in general, not every story has a happy ending and there will be occasions (though mercifully few) when there will be no need for further protracted 'rescue attempts', since it is clear that the individual is beyond resuscitation. In such cases you have no choice but to do what has to be done, and to do it quickly.

Yet even so painful a process as terminating an individual's employment can be carried through in a manner which pays due respect to his or her human dignity. It is a time, not for hypocritical expressions of regret (for you both recognise the inevitability of the situation), but for sincere good wishes for the future, coupled with any final constructive suggestions you may have to offer regarding possible employment opportunities. And unless there are any pressing reasons why the employee should work out his notice, he or she should be paid off and allowed to go. This permits more time not only for job-hunting, but also for reflection about such matters as whether it would be better to be self-employed or whether a change of career would be practicable.

Divesting yourself of people who no longer measure up to your performance standards is one of the most challenging of all managerial tasks, demanding a complex mixture of firmness and compassion. At a time when it can sometimes be tempting to take the soft option and simply hope for some miraculous cure, every wise manager should remember the old saying: 'problems don't go away, they only get worse'. Consider: poor performers can block opportunities for talented high-flyers; take decisions which lose customers and undermine profitability; and, through their incompetence, jeopardise your own promotion prospects. It is not a question of lacking compassion. If you wish to survive you have no choice but to act.

Chapter 8

MASTERING THE APPRAISAL INTERVIEW

Sometimes you retreat, sometimes you attack – but always retain your self-control.

The fact that the vast majority of performance appraisals are a waste of time, that they are inefficient, inaccurate, unfair and corrupt, in no way diminishes their importance: they exist and must therefore be coped with. True, many executives appraise their subordinates with significantly less care than they would exercise in choosing a tie. No matter. Once the appraisal finds its way into your personal file, it becomes part of that 'documentation', so beloved of the personnel bureaucrats, which can affect the course of your future career.

Make no mistake: though they have about as much intellectual validity as a newspaper horoscope (to which they sometimes bear an uncanny resemblance), appraisals *matter*. Those banal comments, those misleading statistics and, above all, those magisterial crosses in the 'merit rating boxes': all may be scrutinised like holy writ when your name is next listed for a promotion vacancy. It is not enough to have done a good job: you must ensure that your achievements are accurately reported. This means mastering the art of the appraisal interview so that it becomes an opportunity instead of an ordeal.

The key to success is to have the right attitude: to come to the interview expecting to hear, not a series of scrupulously fair judgements from a latter-day Solomon, but rather a number of superficial generalities from a highly fallible human being. Most bosses approach the appraisal interview with about as much enthusiasm as a visit to the dentist. Despite the fact that it is you who is being judged, any tension in the situation will be pretty evenly distributed.

— *Having the right strategy* —

Recognise from the start that, as with any other type of interview, personal chemistry is far more important than fact. One of the wilder claims of the management-by-objectives school of appraisal theorists was that MBO-style appraisals would eliminate personal prejudice and usher in a new era of clinically-accurate assessments, based upon 'objective results'. The fact that the interpretation of 'results' remains an intensely personal process was conveniently overlooked.

Instead of expecting the facts to 'speak for themselves' and allowing yourself to be drawn into futile arguments, focus your energies on making it easy for the appraiser to do his or her job. Appraisers are often nervous, so put them at ease. They dislike being critical, so encourage them to be frank. They may not have thought much about your next job move, so let them know what you are looking for. They may know nothing about management training, so help them by suggesting some possible courses.

The most important thing is to look upon the appraiser as neither a friend nor an enemy, but as a *resource*: someone from whom you can learn and who, properly handled, can advance your career. However satisfying it may be for your ego to have outpointed your boss in a verbal duel, it really is a very dubious sort of victory: in business it is the Goliaths, not the Davids, who win. By refusing to score points which could cost you dear in the long run, you are far more likely to end up, not merely with a favourable appraisal, but with the gratitude, albeit hidden, of a much-relieved boss.

Winning through losing

Nothing has done more to devalue the credibility of politicians than their absurd pretence that they are always right and that their opponents' arguments are always wrong. Yet many managers approach their appraisal interviews feeling that they are expected to defend themselves against attack and that if they do not do so, they will be seen as lacking in 'leadership'. Armed to the teeth with facts and figures, they vigorously reject even the mildest criticism as though it were an affront to their managerial virility. Such people are not only extremely tiresome. They ring down the curtain upon their own careers.

Don't try to defend the indefensible: this is the first great commandment of the appraisal interview. Far from exhibiting 'toughness', a person who refuses to admit mistakes (or, worse still, tries to throw the blame upon others) is advertising a monumental managerial immaturity which augurs badly for his or her promotion prospects. Don't try to cover up your mistakes: *learn from them*. Instead of wasting time in generating futile verbal smokescreens, enlist your boss' help in analysing why the error occurred, and how it might be prevented from happening again. Remember: even good performers make mistakes, but rarely the same ones twice.

Such a positive attitude to criticism will tend to disarm – and impress – even the most demanding boss. Apart from relieving him or her from the possibility of an unpleasant wrangle, it will demonstrate your willingness to learn from your boss' experience: a subtle tribute to any superior. A similar point arises when it is the boss who is partly to blame for what has gone wrong, provided that the issue involved is a relatively minor one. Whereas the tyro manager may be tempted to score a few easy points, the more far-sighted performer will ignore such an opening. Many bosses will, of course, acknowledge their faults, but even those who don't will admire your restraint. In business, by losing the odd skirmish or two, you can often end up by winning the war.

Showing your claws

Nevertheless, this doesn't mean that the road to the top is always paved with moral cowardice: there will be many occasions when you must be prepared to stand up for yourself. For example, in the case of a major disaster where, say, a major customer has been lost, or money and resources have been almost criminally wasted, resist any attempt to make you the 'fall guy' for the incompetence of others, including your boss. If you remain silent, your reputation in the company will never recover and even if you succeed in keeping your job, your promotion prospects will be virtually nil.

The time to blow the whistle is a matter of fine judgment: timing is all. Move too soon and your forebodings will be dismissed as 'negative thinking'. Leave it until after the catastrophe has occurred and you will be asked why you didn't speak up sooner. And it will not look too good for your image as a leader if you simply claim to have been following orders. Your loyalty to the company is expected to come first.

The appraisal interview provides you with an ideal opportunity to alert your boss to some impending disaster or, if he or she is personally involved, to indicate that you have no intention of taking all the blame. In either situation you will need to marshal your facts effectively so that your conclusions become well-nigh irresistible. Remember, however, that logic alone may not be enough to save you when the storm finally breaks. It is all too easy for a weak or unscrupulous boss to disclaim all knowledge of your warnings, and to leave you facing charges of gross incompetence.

There is no need to take such a pointless risk: simply set down the facts in a well-argued memorandum and send it to your boss as a record of your discussion (keep several copies for possible future readers). While the tone of your comments should be low-key and unemotional, make it absolutely clear what you believe needs to be done. After all, this is no time for being half-hearted. If the worst should happen, you could be out of a job.

Squeezing the lemon

If you have an appraisal interview without having quizzed your boss about your career development, then you will have missed a splendid chance to engineer some opportunities to broaden your experience and sharpen your skills. Make no mistake: however much management theorists may deplore it, most bosses give very little thought to the development of their subordinates. Constantly under pressure and often worried about their own careers, many abdicate their responsibilities to the personnel department which, in turn, may be painfully slow to act, if indeed it bothers to act at all. It is no use fulminating against the lack of a 'system'. It is basically up to *you* to manage your career.

The way to win your boss' support for some further development activities is not to make arrogant-sounding demands to be sent on expensive outside training courses, but to demonstrate how he or she will benefit from your becoming more accomplished. If, for example, the boss has pointed out some shortcomings in your performance, ask for some suggestions as to how you might overcome them. Better still, anticipate such criticisms and have some ideas of your own, which could range from attending a formal training course to persuading the boss to give you a special assignment or project. What matters is whether you are learning something which is relevant to your needs, not whether you are going on a course with an impressive title which could turn out to be a complete waste of time.

Important though it is, involving the boss in your development strategy is only one element in what ought to be a highly productive discussion about your future. Now is the moment for you to make some firm commitments to developing yourself in your own personal time; for showing your boss that you are willing, indeed eager, to assume responsibility for managing your own development. It may mean enrolling for a correspondence course or for some evening classes, or simply undertaking a planned reading programme of relevant books and journals. No matter. What really counts is that you will have shown your superior that you are a self-motivated individual who tries to make things happen, and that you are keen to take advice from more experienced people.

The appraisal interview also provides an excellent opportunity to discuss the kind of 'structural' problems which prevent many jobholders from being as effective as they might be. Poorly-defined responsibilities, vague reporting relationships, inadequate authority: these are just a few of the more common problems which can undermine even the most talented performer. Once again, present your ideas lucidly and back them up with plenty of examples which will persuade your boss to take speedy action. Remember: it is very much in his or her interests that such problems are overcome. Responsibilities can be delegated, but *not* accountability. For any boss at any level, to develop others is to help oneself.

— *Gimme, gimme* —

It is often tempting when things have gone well at an appraisal interview to 'strike while the iron is hot' and make a direct bid for more pay or early promotion. *Resist these siren voices*: such crassness will invariably prove counter-productive.

It is not merely that nearly all large and many smaller companies operate personnel policies which frown upon the discussion of salaries at appraisal interviews. By making such a brazen attempt to capitalise upon a favourable appraisal, you risk projecting yourself as a crude opportunist whose sense of propriety is sadly lacking. Worse still, you may well embarrass your boss who may not yet have reached a decision about your next pay increase, and will resent your attempts to force the pace. Unless the boss directly initiates a discussion on pay – an unlikely event in all except the small family-run firm – you will just have to be patient. Most companies have long since realised that any potential benefits of the appraisal interview – never very tangible at the best of times – are likely to be completely wiped out by mixing discussions about performance with decisions about pay. A highly emotive subject like money is best discussed at a separate meeting instead of being allowed to deflect attention from the main purpose of the meeting: to motivate the employee to improve his or her performance.

Similarly, common sense should tell you that you are not going to be promoted on the spot, however good your results. The claims of other candidates must be considered and the company's promotion procedures given a chance to work. Nevertheless, while it is naïve to expect a direct cause-and-effect relationship between appraisal and promotion (or, for that matter, between appraisal and pay), this does not mean that you should be reluctant to ask questions about future career opportunities; you most certainly should. And even though your boss may not be able to field some of these questions, it will certainly motivate him or her to discuss them with Personnel and, hopefully, to prepare more carefully for future appraisal interviews. Nor should you be reluctant to spell out those specific jobs which you have your eye on, or even to explore the possibilities of moving into a different function. So long as you convey keenness and ambition, and do so tactfully, there is every reason for you to make clear your aspirations, and to ensure that they are recorded on the appraisal form.

Getting tough

What should be your response if you are convinced that your appraisal is grossly unfair, and that your boss is using the system to blacken your name in the company? Do nothing? Resign? Have a shouting match? Or quietly begin looking for another job?

Frankly, if your relationship has sunk to such depths, it may be beyond repair, whatever you do. However, it is almost always better to discuss your feelings openly with your boss than to rely upon other people for post-appraisal 'justice'. After all, it may be that there is some fundamental misunderstanding waiting to be uncovered which, like an abcess, has poisoned your relations. Once lanced and with normal communications restored, the bitterness of the past may be forgiven and forgotten.

However, if the meeting proves a failure, and you feel that the issues involved justify such a drastic step, then go ahead and seek an appointment with your boss' boss or, alternatively, with a senior personnel manager. And make sure that you can make your charges stick, which means being able to produce plenty of believable examples. After that, there is absolutely no telling how things will go. If you succeed in convincing the 'judge' that right is on your side, then you could (for a time) be the toast of the company. But if you fail, you may well have to pay the price. You could be squeezed out of your job in a matter of weeks.

In the final analysis, only you can answer the key question: 'Is this company so rich in opportunities that I'm prepared to grin and bear it?'. Before you 'point the gun' at your boss, either during or after an appraisal interview, it is a question to which you should know the answer.

While appraisals are invariably one of the least-loved features of a company's personnel policies, nevertheless you should learn to take them seriously. Not to do so is to take unnecessary risks and to hand your rivals a competitive advantage. So play the game for all you are worth. You have nothing to lose except a little self-respect.

Chapter 9

RUNNING SUCCESSFUL MEETINGS

Think of meetings as games of chess – the more familiar your opponents the more predictable their moves.

It's no good resenting meetings or regarding them as a waste of time, a tiresome distraction from the job of managing. They are a vital communications tool, a mechanism through which you make things happen. And unless you know how to use them properly, you are unlikely ever to fulfil your potential.

Every meeting is a piece of theatre, a scriptless play where the actors make up their lines as they go along. This does not mean that there is no plot: indeed there may be several. It simply means that when the characters speak, they may be less than frank in disclosing their motives. But rest assured there is *always* a motive. No contribution is ever wholly without purpose.

This chapter deals with what it takes to run effective meetings, a key component of your leadership role. The way that you handle yourself and others, the drive you display in getting things done, your skill in defusing personality clashes: these are stepping stones on that golden road which leads to the boardroom and an MD's chair. The skills involved are well worth mastering.

Running a successful meeting depends upon whether you have clear objectives and are determined to get results. The sooner that this becomes clear to your colleagues, the sooner they will begin to contribute effectively.

— Establishing control —

People who make their mark at meetings owe their success to two key factors: good preparation and persuasive communication. To have done your homework properly – to have collected, digested and evaluated all the relevant information on a given subject – is a prime requirement of the top-flight chairperson, and is certain to command a measure of respect. Many people who chair meetings cannot be bothered to familiarise themselves with every major item on the agenda. They 'fight their corner' when their pet issue comes up, and thereafter relapse into a kind of coma which is only broken by the arrival of tea.

The skilled chairperson makes no such mistake. Reports are read, memos memorised, facts marshalled and arguments deployed for maximum impact. The effect of all this mental preparation is like that of weight training upon the professional boxer. Optimism blooms, self-confidence surges and there is every chance of a successful outcome.

Nevertheless, as every salesperson knows, having a good case is not enough: what matters is the skill with which you present it. Facts, like clay on a potter's wheel, must be shaped to suit the meeting's requirements, particularly those members who carry the most weight. It will help, of course, if before the meeting you have lobbied for support on a key proposal, instead of hoping that things will turn out all right. But whether or not you have taken out such insurance, try always to anticipate the opposing arguments. By demolishing such resistance with style and flair, you are bound to impress any uncommitted listeners who will then make haste to jump on your bandwagon. But never humiliate someone who opposes you. Today's enemy could be tomorrow's friend.

Sometimes you may find yourself having to take over a meeting which is nominally being run by a more senior executive. Faced with a weak, vacillating leader who is totally incapable of making up his or her mind – and with a vital proposal in danger of being lost – you may have no alternative but to seize the reins. Nevertheless, however strongly you may feel about your project, make it easy for the chairperson to step aside, and for others to accept your temporary leadership. This is best achieved by being courteous to everyone, especially the person whom you have temporarily 'deposed'. Once you have won the argument and your proposal has been accepted, resume your role as an ordinary member of the meeting. The chairperson is unlikely to feel humiliated, nor will your colleagues resent your actions. They are far more likely to admire your initiative in bringing the meeting back on course.

Handling awkward members

Some people look upon meetings as a kind of extended coffee break, a welcome diversion from boring routine. Others fume with impatience throughout every discussion, visibly wishing that they were back in their offices, and muttering ill-temperedly during long-winded contributions. Yet another group takes refuge in being half-asleep, dreaming peacefully of the coming weekend while the verbal battles rage around them. The chairperson, however, must appear both alert and interested. It can sometimes be a most punishing task.

Fortunately, most meetings have at least one member, invariably male, who can be relied upon to keep the chairperson awake. Most abundant of this dismal breed are The Ramblers, discursive mega-bores who, if unchecked, can wreck any discussion with their interminable waffling. There is no point in mollycoddling these masters of tedium; they are far too insensitive to take a hint. The only way to curb them is to jump in quickly when they pause for breath, and pose a new question for the whole group to discuss. Be assured that your efforts will not be resented. It is the over-polite chairperson who tends to lose face.

Almost equally tiresome is the pedantic Boffin, technical specialist and jargon-mongerer for whom English is virtually a foreign tongue. Attaching but little importance to clear communication, since it would only tend to dispel the 'mystique', Boffins are a menace to any chairperson, since they are chiefly concerned with showing off. The surest way to deflate their egos is to keep on asking them to use simpler terms 'so that we can understand what you are talking about'. The more frequent and tetchier your interventions, the greater will be the deflationary effect. Once again, your actions will be extremely popular. After all, it is one thing to be carried away by one's enthusiasm; quite another to be a patronising bore.

The third most numerous of these meetings pests are The Windbags. Brothers-in-boredom of the bumbling Ramblers, Windbags are men for whom talking is a kind of drug, a habit to which they are hopelessly addicted. Infinitely pompous and incapable of brevity, they pose a lethal threat to any meeting, since, if unchallenged, they will dominate the discussion, and make it impossible to get anything done. The 'treatment' for The Windbag is much the same as for The Rambler, though it can often pay to talk to him before the meeting, and request him to keep his comments as succinct as possible. If that fails, as it sometimes will, intervene sharply and summarise his point. Then move on quickly to someone else. Waves of approval will break all around you.

Much more formidable than this verbose trio are The Toughies, loud-voiced bullies who delight in intimidating insecure chairpersons with their scathing invective and explosive tantrums. The reason for their obnoxious behaviour is that they regard all meetings as a waste of time, and would much rather be back in their offices, cracking the whip over their luckless subordinates. While you can often succeed in neutralising Toughies by skilfully flattering their outsize egos, there will come a time when you will have no choice but to 'shoot it out' in front of everyone. When this happens, do not hesitate: shoot to kill. Tell the offender to either improve his behaviour or leave the meeting. And make sure that you send for him after the meeting and tell him how unacceptable his conduct is. Having to 'lay it on the line' can be highly unpleasant, but sometimes you really have no alternative. You either act decisively or lose your credibility. It is one of those challenges that you *have* to accept.

Building the right atmosphere

Ideally, meetings should be a team effort, a collective focussing upon common objectives. Yet all too often they end in irritation and confusion, with cynicism rampant and self-interest supreme. Instead of leaving the meeting with a clear sense of purpose, members mutter angrily about 'time-wasting waffle' and swap interpretations as to what has been decided. The more frequent such meetings the more that morale suffers and the worse the effect upon business results.

As the chairperson of a meeting, your job is to provide leadership: to clarify objectives and to secure commitment. Far from running the meeting as a one-man band, your task is to ensure that everyone participates in what ought to be a collaborative process, not a dreary exercise in autocratic management. And the only way you can convince people that you mean what you say is to show that you are influenced by their contributions: it is your decisions, not your intentions, which determine your credibility. But first you must create an atmosphere in which people are willing to speak their minds, and to do so openly, without fear of the consequences.

While there are no overnight panaceas for creating trust, there are a few golden rules which, if you persist in applying them, will bring results. First, no matter how strongly you may feel about an issue, never start a discussion with a forceful statement of your personal views; if you give the impression that your mind is made up, why should people bother to change it? Far better to outline the issue in a general way and then invite contributions on a specific aspect. By listening to the discussion without constantly interrupting and by taking notes on points of interest, you will demonstrate to everyone that you value their inputs, and that they have a real opportunity to influence your thinking. When you summarise the discussion and give your decision, it will be clear that you have been influenced by others' experience. There is no surer way of encouraging people to contribute and of tapping the creativity of the whole of the group.

Nevertheless, there are plenty of things that can go wrong during a heated discussion, and you must stay in control or forfeit your leadership role. This doesn't mean that you should become alarmed when strong feelings are expressed, and rush in quickly to damp them down; such emotions are a tribute to the relaxed atmosphere you have created. Essentially your task is to ensure that valuable ideas are not lost in the cut-and-thrust of a vigorous debate, and that the discussion itself does not become repetitive. Your principal weapon is, of course, the summary, and by using it skilfully you can achieve three important goals. First, you can bring the discussion back on course and restore its sense of purpose; second, you can highlight those areas where there is general agreement; and finally, and most important of all, you can announce your decision, allocate responsibility and set a deadline for completion of the task. It is a mistake to leave the communication of decisions to the end of what may have been a long and tiring meeting. Far better to use your summary to spell out your decision while the topic is fresh in everyone's mind.

Maintaining the momentum

The success of a meeting can depend on its pace. A change of tempo – speeding up or slowing down – is often desirable to keep up the momentum. The more that you can succeed in infecting others with your enthusiasm, the more likely the meeting will achieve its objectives. But you may have to work hard to infuse some variety into what can easily degenerate into dull routine.

Don't be afraid to use visual aids; charts, films and sketches can all help to reinforce your key points. In particular, always have a flipchart available and use it constantly. Not only will it help you to keep track of the discussion and to refer to points made earlier, but it can be absolutely indispensable when you are doing your summaries, and will help to focus everyone's attention.

Make sure that the participants listen to each other. If you think that someone has been misunderstood or not heard, ask the individual to repeat the point or, better still, ask a listener to repeat what he or she heard. You can also help the less effective communicators by paraphrasing their main points, using simple, down-to-earth words. Never let people get away with vague or ambiguous statements: unchecked, they can slow down a discussion and stifle creativity. If things become tedious, jump in quickly with a timely summary and then move on to another issue. Once a meeting loses its momentum, it can be extremely difficult to rekindle enthusiasm.

Stamp on negative thinking. There will always be at least one person at every meeting who will tell you that something can't be done or that someone would be upset or that there are insufficient resources to complete the task. The vast majority of these Jeremiahs are people who are afraid of change and want only to be left alone in their comfortable ruts, marking time until their retirement. Make it clear that such attitudes are unacceptable, and that problems exist to be overcome, not treated as though they were insuperable obstacles. If this advice should seem unduly harsh, remember that defeatism is highly contagious, and can spread like wildfire if it is not dealt with promptly. You cannot afford to tolerate an infection which could seriously undermine the group's will to win.

Remember, too, that the loudness or softness of your voice will also have an effect on the meeting. Try to avoid speaking in a monotone; raise or lower your voice, depending on what you want to emphasise. In short, use your voice to change the pace and mood of the meeting, and don't be afraid to use humour to keep everyone relaxed. After all, *you* are the pace-setter. It is your example which sets the pattern for others' behaviour.

Finally, there is no iron law which says that you have to have a regular meeting on the same day of the month or at the same place and time; though sameness is welcomed by some, it is boring to others. Why not vary the meeting place and time to suit different members of the group? Or ask the group where and when they'd like to meet next time? And if the meeting lasts for a whole day or longer, and the members keep going back to the same seats after every break, suggest they change and sit next to someone else. Variety helps to make a meeting tick.

Running a meeting is a test of your teambuilding skills. In essence, the challenge is to transform a group of individuals into an effective team with everyone pulling in the same direction. Sometimes, however, you may be confronted with highly-charged emotional issues which may threaten to prevent you from achieving your goal. For example, if certain individuals behave in a hostile way to one another, it is important to talk to them about their hostility, and try to achieve a measure of understanding. Once you have done this, you can get on with the job of building your team. But you can only build effectively on a sound foundation. And the soundest foundation is your *personal leadership*.

Chapter 10

MAKING EFFECTIVE PRESENTATIONS

Learn the skills of speaking – every leader needs them.

Being able to deliver effective presentations, particularly in the setting of a major company conference, is one of the surest ways of attracting attention and of establishing yourself as a person to watch. In an age when front-rank politicians and City moguls vie with each other in oratorical dreariness, those who can master the speaker's art have a distinct advantage over those who cannot. In American companies, in particular, executives who can make the pursuit of profit sound like a quest for the Holy Grail are hugely admired. And there are few organisations where a stylish eloquence will not at least ensure a respectful hearing for whatever ideas you are putting forward.

This chapter does not deal in depth with the *techniques* of making effective presentations (voice, eye contact, mannerisms, etc.); these can best be learned on a formal course under the expert guidance of a skilled instructor. But no amount of training in techniques will compensate for poor attitudes and ineffectual strategies; speaking is about confidence, not confidence tricks. Once you have won your internal battle against fear of failure, you can begin to graft on those specialist skills which will give your presentations a professional gloss. You must also learn how to package your material so that it gleams with relevance for a particular audience.

Overcoming fear

Why so many speakers should fear those whom they are addressing remains a mystery of human nature, wholly irrational yet very real. In truth, it is the audience which has most to fear, since there are few more painful experiences in life than to have to listen to some droning bore from whose nerve-jangling utterances there is no escape. For unlike a television programme which, if it displeases, can be switched off, the dreadful presentation must be endured. One can hardly walk out without eyebrows being raised, and there is a limit to the number of times that illness can be feigned.

The fact is that the audience has a powerful vested interest in hearing a good presentation, one which clarifies complex issues and fires the imagination with interesting new ideas. Why, then, do some speakers act as though their listeners were hungry lions, waiting to pounce on the slightest error and to tear them apart with awkward questions? The answer lies in such speakers' fears of making fools of themselves and – if senior management are present – of permanently damaging their promotion prospects. The first is a question of lack of self-confidence, the second a delusion of over-stressed minds.

Nevertheless, since the mind is a kind of battleground in which both positive and negative aspects struggle for supremacy, your task is to help the white knight of optimism slay the dragon of despair. The best way of doing this is to use the technique of 'visioning': to imagine yourself giving a successful presentation and positively revelling in the whole experience. Think of yourself at the podium, totally in command of your material and presenting it with a drive and enthusiasm which the audience finds completely irresistible. Imagine the upturned faces hanging on your every word, the appreciative laughter at your subtle quips, the heads nodding in agreement as you punch home your points. Revel in the waves of applause as you resume your seat, bask in the chairman's compliments and hear yourself dealing masterfully with respectful questioners. Not least, when the meeting is over, see yourself accepting your colleagues' congratulations and receiving yet more praise from senior management.

There is nothing fanciful about this approach; it is based upon how people motivate themselves. Those who lack self-confidence, who feel that they will never be good speakers, will tend to fulfil their own defeatist prophecies. Those who are determined to succeed, and are driven by a vision of what success could mean, will push themselves to achieve their dream. As the saying goes, 'it's all in the mind'. Techniques, though important, are not nearly enough.

Preparing effectively

Presentations are like battles: they demand good planning and preparation. Those speakers who hope that it will be 'all right on the night', and neglect to prepare themselves properly, are simply proclaiming their lack of professionalism. They ought not to be surprised when they are coolly received. Audiences resent their time being wasted.

The cornerstone of any effective presentation is a clean-cut objective; without it there will be no unifying force and even good material will lose much of its impact. Good objectives, however, are not just plucked out of the air. They always represent some kind of compromise between what the speaker wants to achieve and what the audience would like to hear. This means that presenters must research their audiences to make sure that they understand their major concerns. And even when you are confident that this is not a problem, it is often worth checking with a few well-informed colleagues that their perceptions are much the same as yours.

Having defined your objective, begin collecting your material. Take a large piece of paper and write down every significant item which could be of use: facts, ideas, opinions, judgements – everything which occurs to you. Give yourself plenty of time for this 'brainstorming' process. If you rush through it too quickly you may realise later on that you have overlooked a number of important facts and ideas which demand to be included, but which will require you virtually to dismantle your presentation. Only when you are sure that you have everything you need should you move on to stage two of the planning process: organising your material into an effective structure.

But what *is* an effective structure? One which positions your material for maximum impact, which means that it must be logical but also *imaginative*. A logical structure is easy to follow, it builds vital bridges between facts and ideas and, above all, it encourages an audience to keep on listening (a confused audience will simply switch off). An imaginative structure is one which reflects *the audience's needs*. It gives most weight (and therefore most time) to those things which concern *this* particular group and makes no attempt to cover every possible aspect. The speaker's hobby-horses are kept firmly in check. Audience satisfaction is the primary goal.

Once you have a framework for your presentation (four to five main headings are usually enough), you can now begin to slot your material into the appropriate pigeon hole. It is at this stage that the time factor comes rushing to the fore. Clearly, having an hour in which to make your presentation is a very different proposition from being restricted to ten minutes; the less time you have, the more vital it becomes to select the right material. Nevertheless, whether you have plenty of time or only a few minutes, the same basic principle applies: divide your material into three main categories. The first is strictly reserved for your 'musts': that select band of critical points which are the driving force of your presentation and must stand out like beacons in the audience's mind. Next comes the 'probables': useful material for fleshing out your main points, but only to be used if time permits. Finally, there are the 'possibles': lightweight material consisting of items such as additional statistics or case histories whose use can only be justified if your time allocation is exceptionally generous.

Rehearsing the presentation

Given that professional actors spend days and often weeks rehearsing their parts in an important play, it is surprising that so few executives try out their presentations, thereby missing opportunities to make worthwhile adjustments. Yet just as an actor gains confidence from familiarity with his lines, so a business presentation will gain in stature if given a professional polish, the result of much heart-searching behind the scenes.

But whereas the vast majority of actors work with a script from which departures are rarely authorised, you, the executive, have a wide range of choices from no notes at all to a typewritten speech. In making your decision, bear in mind one of the golden rules of effective speaking: the more spontaneous and natural you sound, the greater your impact. This, of course, argues for fewer notes since the more voluminous they are the stronger will be the temptation to read them. Nevertheless, to eschew notes completely, and to rely upon the inspiration of the moment, is a high-risk strategy for all except the most gifted speaker.

The solution, predictably, lies in a compromise which avoids both the nightmarish prospect of 'drying up' without any notes to fall back on and that profound audience boredom which is the certain consequence of reading from a script. Whether you use postcards containing just a few main headings – a technique frequently recommended on training courses – or whether you are happier with slightly fuller notes, is not all that important. What *does* matter is whether your notes are in a *usable* form. It is far from impressive to an audience to be addressed by a speaker who spends a great deal of time clearly trying to decipher his or her notes. Notes must be legible or they are useless.

Having taken out whatever level of insurance, in the form of notes, that makes you feel confident and secure, you are almost ready to begin rehearsing. But there is one last decision to be made: will you be needing any visual aids? While there is no doubt that some visual aids are grossly over-used, reducing the presentation to little more than a peep-show, it is nonetheless true that, judiciously selected, they can add variety and colour to the spoken word. For communicating certain types of information, notably complex financial and technical data, they are totally indispensable; here it is perfectly true that 'one picture is worth a thousand words'. But, equally, there are few more chilling sights than the speaker who marches to the podium carrying a vast pile of transparencies which he then proceeds to show at the rate of about six a minute! This kind of visual overkill merely confuses and irritates an audience which begins to feel patronised by being forced to look at so many unnecessary pictures. Remember, the more selective you are in your use of visuals the greater their impact. Using them indiscriminately breeds apathy and boredom.

Now, at last, you can begin to rehearse, and, once again, there is a good deal of scope for individual preferences. Some speakers like to rehearse alone at home, aided perhaps by a tape recorder or an even more revealing full-length mirror. Others seek the frank opinions of their spouses or partners or a few close colleagues at work whose judgements they value. It is not so much a question of becoming word-perfect as knowing the structure of your talk and what the key points are under each main heading. It is rather like starting out on a car journey. The more that you study the route beforehand, the less likely you are to make a mistake.

Listening to yourself on the tape recorder, watching yourself in the mirror, listening to the comments of your friendly 'critics': all are ways of obtaining valuable feedback which can enable you to strengthen your presentation. As with other types of criticism, don't waste time resenting it; *learn from it*. After all, if these are comments which are made by your friends, there is every chance that others will agree with them.

Finally, make sure that your visual equipment is in tip-top condition, and that you know how to operate it. Many a presenter has been thrown by the failure of a bulb which 'pops' the instant he switches on the overhead projector. Check your equipment *before* the presentation.

Handling questions

Having given your presentation, you face the final hurdle of answering questions. Anticipating the more obvious questions and preparing well thought-out answers is, of course, an essential part of the planning process. But what matters just as much as the content of your replies is your facial expression and tone of voice; in short, the quality of your *social skills*.

Here, as in every other aspect of effective speaking, your mental attitudes are all-important. If you persist in behaving like a fugitive from justice, eyes roving desperately around the room, and mumbling your replies instead of sounding confident, the audience may conclude that you have something to hide, and may well decide to find out what it is. It is at this point that various well-known types of questioner begin to emerge: The Nit-Picker, who tries to trip you up over some trivial statistic; The Bully with his intimidating roar; The Knifeman with his cruel sense of humour; The Bore whose interminable question turns into a speech. With all of these inquisitors, no matter how great the provocation, you must resolve to keep your temper and to treat them courteously. If you can literally keep smiling and retain your composure, you are sure to win the audience's respect, and there is every chance that some of them will spring to your defence.

But whether your questioners are friendly or hostile, you must visualise them as *customers* whose needs must be satisfied. This is where your body-language can be so important. The attentive posture while the question is being asked; the ready smile when the questioner makes a joke; the impassive reaction to a telling thrust or a cutting comment; such behaviour demonstrates your coolness under fire, a prime requirement for a top-flight executive. This is why making presentations figures so prominently in those elaborate 'assessment centres', whereby companies attempt to identify their future top managers. The qualities involved in commanding an audience's attention and in dealing authoritatively with difficult questions lie right at the heart of the leadership role. After all, if leaders are to communicate their vision of the future, they must be prepared to led from the front, not abdicate their responsibilities to the PR department.

Like any other skill, making presentations requires plenty of practice; hence the importance of attending a good training course where you will be given an insight into the tricks of the trade. But effective speaking is much more than a bundle of techniques. It requires a determination to excel as a communicator: to transmit a message which you consider important and to do so with all the enthusiasm you can muster. If you can persuade the audience of the strength of your convictions, you are more than half-way to a successful presentation. Without such commitment, techniques will fail. To sell your message, you must first sell yourself.

Part III

Politics is the test

Confound their politics
Frustrate their knavish tricks.

Henry Carey, God Save the King

Chapter 11

AVOIDING THOSE KILLER MISTAKES

Never violate the organisation's unwritten rules – or you'll remain forever an outcast from the tribe.

Companies are like icebergs: it's what lies beneath the surface that really counts. Despite the efforts of the professional image-builders, it takes more than a change of logo to change a company's values, for its 'culture', like Rome, was not built in a day. Every organisation, large or small, public or private, evolves its own way of looking at the world, a reflection of the views of its founding fathers which continue to influence not only business decisions, but also the way that employees behave.

Failure to comply with these unwritten rules can have a serious effect upon an executive's progress, however competent he or she may otherwise be. Sometimes, as in many family-owned firms, the rules are clear-cut and down-to-earth, for whatever your rank, you are in essence a family retainer charged with carrying out the family's bidding. But in the larger organisations, life is more complicated, and the behavioural minefields more skilfully concealed. Nevertheless, there are some kinds of conduct which are sure to be criticised even in the most liberal-minded concern.

Every ambitious executive needs a behavioural map of the organisation in which he or she works. To a newcomer, that map will seem vague and incomplete, providing only the sketchiest information. But, with time and experience, these mists will clear and he will learn to negotiate even the most daunting obstacles.

Gatecrashing

Animals mark their territories and so do executives, their principal tools being job descriptions which act in effect as garden fences, defining the boundaries between different jobs. The stronger the grip of job descriptions the easier it is for the unwary newcomer to blunder unwittingly into someone else's territory, thus risking attack by an angry colleague who is outraged by this threat to his or her status and security.

In the kind of firm where bureaucracy is rampant, there are few greater sins than to appear to be usurping a colleague's authority. It is seen as a recipe for the kind of organisational anarchy which invariably results in jobs being lost. No wonder that when an intruder is detected, a whole range of counter-measures are automatically triggered. Memos, like missiles, speed towards the offending executive, demanding unconditional surrender and immediate withdrawal. Should they be ignored, then even heavier weapons are brought into play: policy manuals, organisation charts and detailed statements of procedures where every paragraph is like an electrified fence designed to discourage illegal entry.

There is no surer way of blotting your copybook than to acquire a reputation as a brazen encroacher upon other people's territory. Like a flock of starlings uniting to drive off a marauding eagle, old rivalries will be forgotten as everyone closes ranks against the common foe. Only the most monarchical of chief executives can hope to change the ground rules without provoking a 'peasants' revolt' among his sullen and affronted subjects. And even he may have to pay a heavy price as morale plummets and good people leave.

Philandering

Love, it's said, makes the world go round, but in business it is seen as a dangerous distraction which seduces executives from the job of managing. Nothing is more likely to immobilise even the most dedicated executive than the grapevine's latest bulletin on some torrid affair between colleagues who may be working a mere stone's throw away. In a world where rationality is a much-prized virtue, the occasional blaze of unbridled passion can provide a most refreshing change from the daily routine, and a first-class antidote to executive stress.

But *not* for the participants. The moment the affair becomes public knowledge, senior brows begin to furrow in the personnel department, and invisible question marks hover over the lovers' careers. It is not so much the morality of their liaison that displeases: it is the potential impact upon their work, plus the distracting effect upon other executives. All the world loves a lover, except top management. There is scant sympathy for those who are judged indiscreet.

If, as often happens, the affair breaks up, it is frequently impossible for those involved to continue working together. The likelihood is that either one or the other will leave, and whoever is left behind will be held responsible. With colleagues taking sides regarding who is to blame, it can sometimes take weeks before things return to normal. Again, it is the executive who has stayed put who becomes the scapegoat, and whose promotion prospects begin to look bleak.

However great the temptation, resist any attempt by your heart to rule your head. Keep your work and your sex life in separate compartments, and find your partners from outside the office. Above all, do not draw so heavily upon your emotional bank account that you arrive at the office drained of energy and lacking the stamina for a full day's work. If you cannot keep your affaires in order, you may be seen as a mere dilettante who lacks the commitment for a top management job.

In short, your relationships with the opposite sex should be friendly and comradely but nonetheless businesslike. Don't allow a question mark to be placed over your maturity by indiscreet behaviour which, rest assured, will soon reach the ears of higher management. Only fools dice with their careers.

— *Leapfrogging* —

Being loyal to the boss is not just an optional extra for ambitious executives: it is a prime requirement for their future success. Once you are perceived as an executive Brutus, ever ready to plunge a dagger into your boss' reputation, windows of opportunity will be smartly closed, and doors leading to promotion slammed in your face.

One of the most resented forms of disloyalty is leapfrogging: going over your boss' head and communicating directly with higher management. Only the boss' prolonged absence from the office or a sudden emergency are seen as justifying such a heinous 'crime', particularly if you are suspected of 'poisoning the well' by revealing details of mistakes and inefficiencies which can only rebound to your boss' discredit. Whether such criticisms are justified or not, your behaviour will be regarded as flagrant disloyalty: a breach of that trust between boss and subordinate without which teamwork becomes a utopian dream.

There are, of course, other forms of leapfrogging which, while not as crude as those described, are equally resented. Adding your boss' boss' name to the circulation list for a memo or report which you have written (usually under that weasel heading 'for information only') is one of the oldest tricks in the book. It is generally used by subordinates who are having difficulty in getting their boss to accept their ideas and are trying to twist his arm by involving his boss. However, any senior manager worthy of his stock options will know how to deal with such blatant carpet-bagging: an icy silence is the most effective response. Even when approached directly by the would-be manipulator during supposedly 'chance' encounters in the car park or in the corridor outside his office, the experienced senior executive will know how to react. A terse 'Discuss it with your boss' will do the trick.

Even though competition for promotion is becoming ever fiercer, to be known as a backstabber will do you no good at all. If you are seen as someone who cannot be trusted, how can you expect others to want you in their teams?

Name-dropping

Any executive who believes that constant name-dropping will smooth his way to the top is living in a vanished world. Whereas 'breeding' and 'background' were once regarded as acceptable substitutes for talent and skill, today's competitive business climate has seen off snobbery and enthroned 'professionalism'.

Nevertheless, lurking in the thickets of the executive jungle, there are still a few dinosaurs who have yet to recognise that knowing the odd peer of the realm or having been at school with the chairman's son is no instant passport to the boardroom. Indeed, in these meritocratic times, those who flaunt their 'connections' are likely to be marked down as 'immature' or 'insecure': weaklings who are using others' fame to divert attention from their own meagre talents.

Making constant favourable references to other companies you have worked for is another form of name-dropping which can cause resentment, especially if you are invariably critical of your present employer. While the *occasional* reference to your experience with another company will not attract criticism – especially if it is relevant to a current problem – continual sneering at the 'stupidity' of your own company's policies is bound to come across as blatant disloyalty. Never forget that some of your colleagues will have invested many years of their lives in working for the company, and will resent being told, in effect, that they have wasted their time. Pride in the company, like pride in the regiment, is a perfectly commendable human emotion. So resist the temptation to make unfavourable comparisons. You cannot risk being seen as a dangerous subversive who owes no loyalty except to himself.

— Ridiculing —

Business is no place for hyper-sensitive individuals, but neither is it a school for trainee sadists nor a playground for satirists with whiplash tongues. While you have every right to defend yourself when the occasion demands, you must learn to be judicious in your choice of weapons.

Sarcasm – especially the cruder, more personalised variety – will gain you nothing except a reputation for downright unpleasantness. Being able to transfix your opponents with stiletto-like phrases may seem a useful executive skill, but victories gained in such a fashion are dearly won. Fear breeds dislike, and dislike can turn to hatred. Once that happens, your hopes of being trusted will vanish forever, and your enemies will delight in publicising your mistakes. Such cooperation as you receive from your colleagues and subordinates will be strictly formal, and there will be a distinct lack of enthusiasm for answering your questions.

The least acceptable use of sarcasm is when it is employed to belittle one's own boss, especially at meetings when other senior people are present. Mercifully rare though such tactics are, they are occasionally utilised by ruthless subordinates (invariably male) who are seeking to demolish their boss' credibility in the hope of being seen as ready-made successors. However, far from signing their superior's death warrant, such crass behaviour has the opposite effect: it makes everyone want to spring to his or her defence. When that happens the offending subordinate may just as well leave the company. Having destroyed his relationship with his current boss, he will discover that every other boss' hand is turned against him.

— Boasting —

It is one thing to take pride in one's achievements, but quite another to keep ramming them down your colleagues' throats. While no one will begrudge you an occasional bout of self-congratulation, if your every utterance is sprinkled with I's, you will soon be written off as a tiresome bore. Worse still, if you persist in claiming that you are right about everything, a kind of mafia will emerge among your colleagues consisting of people who are determined to puncture your ego. This may even result in the occasional practical joke, such as a fictitious invitation to have lunch with the chairman.

Like his blood-brother The Name-Dropper, The Boaster is high on self-love but low on self-knowledge. The least attractive of the species is the out-and-out materialist with a significant private income who flaunts his prosperity like some latter-day Midas. Constant references to villas in Spain, gourmet restaurants and high-performance cars are scarcely calculated to endear him to colleagues who may be grappling with school fees, mortgages and astronomical bills for house repairs. Nothing arouses that sleeping giant, Envy, more quickly than a person who appears immune to those financial slings and arrows which buffet the vast majority of the human race. Not least those who work in business.

Crawling

The days are long gone when businesses could be run as feudal kingdoms, with managers holding life-or-death powers over their subordinates' careers. Today progressive companies everywhere recognise that high-calibre people will not tolerate being bullied and, if they continue to be mismanaged, will take their talents elsewhere. Modern executives see themselves as captains of teams, not as not-so-distant relatives of Genghis Khan.

But all of this is lost upon The Crawlers, people who, psychologically speaking, are always on their knees. Convinced that the ability to grovel is the passport to success, there is no act of flattery or of self-humiliation which is beyond the repertoire of these human doormats. Determined to curry favour with those who 'matter', they are the ones whose Christmas cards to the boss are always outrageously expensive; who are first in line with glutinous flattery after even the most mediocre presentation; and who are always hoping that the boss' car will break down so that they can promptly offer a lift home. After all, what is a 30-mile detour compared with such a golden opportunity to ingratiate oneself?

Sadly, all too many executives prove vulnerable to the wiles of these fawning schemers, and start believing the nonsense with which they are so assiduously fed. The results are predictable: The Crawler is promoted, good people leave, the department begins to disintegrate and The Crawler (still fawning) has to be replaced. What a ridiculously high price to pay for tolerating such tricksters! Like weevils in a granary, they form a kind of enemy within.

— *Brick-dropping* —

There are many occasions in an executive's career when he will have an equal opportunity either to shine or to damage his prospects, and occasionally such damage may be terminal. Some errors, however, are relatively minor, and will be quickly forgiven and forgotten: the visiting speaker at a conference whose name you mispronounce while introducing him; the slightly off-colour joke which annoys a female colleague; the overseas customer who expects you to meet him at the airport and has to wait half an hour because you have underestimated the rush-hour traffic. Certainly such situations can be embarrassing, but a fulsome and sincere apology will generally soothe even the most ruffled feathers. But there are other wounds which do not heal so easily.

Not surprisingly, many of these situations have a common factor: drink. It is all too easy during a convivial cocktail hour before an important company dinner – and even more so during the dinner itself – to take that 'one drink too many' which can cause you to lose control. Gripped by a mood of alcoholic euphoria which seems destined to last forever, laughing immoderately at the feeblest quip, calling for your glass to be refilled at ever-diminishing intervals, it is here that you can attract the wrong sort of attention from senior people who may be several drinks behind you, and are still very much sober. Should your subsequent conduct result in widespread embarrassment – a rambling, incoherent after-dinner speech, a wine glass knocked over a lady guest's dress – then you can expect a severe tongue-lashing when you are next in the office, particularly if your behaviour has been witnessed by VIP visitors.

The remedy is clear: know your limits as a drinker and stay well within them. Remember, too, that bars have ears and that any indiscreet comments about your boss and his policies may well reach him or her via some notorious company gossip who may be standing only a few feet away. A shrewd executive never loses control, for it takes only a few tactless moments to shatter the achievements of years, and to make any future progress highly problematical.

Finally, never forget that, in addition to these general prohibitions, every organisation is likely to have other specific philosophies and other preferred modes of behaviour which, taken together, add up to 'the way we do things around here'. Find out what they are, and find out quickly. In business the prizes go not only to the talented, but also to the best-informed.

Chapter 12

DEALING WITH OFFICE POLITICIANS

Some business games can be lethal – either play to win or don't get involved.

There are two kinds of business games: the ones you play at business school or on management training courses and the ones which you play in your own organisation either to defend or to sell yourself. Make no mistake: in any organisation where people are seeking to extend or to protect their influence, there will always be a political dimension. Man, as Aristotle pointed out long ago, is a *political* animal. He will always struggle for his place in the sun.

Essentially, office politics is part of the selling game, of that process of *persuasion* which goes on in all organisations at all levels at all times. It can be a force for good or a force for evil. It can result in efficient or inefficient people rising to the top, depending upon how well they play the game. Instead of bewailing the existence of a political factor in business, ambitious executives focus on two main areas: first, how to project themselves and their ideas most effectively; second, how to thwart those who 'play dirty': rivals who try to wreck their careers with various perfidious ploys and strategies.

Backstabbing

This is perhaps the most common (and certainly the most obvious) of all 'dirty tricks'. It simply involves spreading some falsehood about you which, if believed, could seriously damage your future prospects. For example, one of your rivals might put it around that you are furious over your boss' rejection of a new idea on which you had set your heart, and that you are in almost daily contact with 'head-hunters' concerning a move to a competitor. Were such a story to be believed, it could speedily result in your removal from all promotion lists since you would appear to be guilty of two cardinal executive sins: disloyalty to the company and 'prima donna-ism': an inability to tolerate disappointments and setbacks.

The only effective way of countering such calumnies is to act decisively as soon as you hear about them (to remain silent will be taken as an admission of guilt). Instead of waiting for a certain chilliness to creep into your boss' manner – a sure sign that the story has reached him – tell him frankly what you have heard and assure him that it's totally without foundation. By employing such a direct approach, you will not only stop the poison spreading further, you will also establish yourself as a fearless straight-shooter whose word is his bond. What more could a boss ask for?

Always do your best to find out the source of the infection; you may find that you have a new rival who has hitherto been lying low, but has now decided to try to spike your guns. Once you have identified the culprit, carry on as normal: there is no point in having an angry confrontation which may dent your reputation for mature behaviour. Nevertheless, let it be known both directly and through your friends that the rumour has been well and truly scotched, and that it was *you* who took the initiative in informing senior management. This will signal to your rivals that you are no mere merchantman but a man o'war bristling with sophisticated weaponry.

While no one likes a backstabber, the sad truth is that they are sometimes believed. Don't feign indifference; put out the fire before it takes a hold.

— *Counterfeiting* —

Every ambitious executive looks for challenge and advancement; money is just a way of measuring progress. It is this urge to go on growing which stands out like a beacon among executive motivators, and makes being promoted such a sought-after prize. But be careful: things are not always as they seem. There may be quicksands in those promising new pastures.

To be blunt, some so-called promotions are just not worth having, especially if they remove you from a mainstream activity and dump you in a staff job with a limited future. Unless such a move is a recognised development assignment with a specific timescale, then fight like fury to stay where you are. The chances are that someone in the personnel department (or on the 'management succession committee') doesn't like you, and has put your name forward to clear the way for one of his own cronies to be promoted to a much bigger job. Needless to say, this vacancy will not be announced until you have accepted the earlier offer.

Joining the wrong sort of task force can also damage your promotion prospects. Unless the MD has given the project his personal support and the team is bursting with recognised company 'stars', it may simply be another attempt to elbow you aside to make way for someone else's 'favourite son'. It will do your career no good whatever to be associated with a group of mediocre performers who are engaged in the pursuit of some unquantifiable benefit which no one cares about anyway. Far better to stay where you are and wait for an opportunity that would *really* make a difference.

The most potentially lethal of these fraudulent 'opportunities' is the offer of a 'senior' job in a small overseas subsidiary, where you risk being forgotten almost as soon as you step off the plane.

Even the glamour of an MD's title will not compensate you for the dubious privilege of presiding over a small, insignificant operation which is, in effect, little more than the branch office of the parent company. Moreover, when disenchantment sets in, and you begin manoeuvring for a return home, your pleas may be ignored. Your competitors may well have increased their influence, and may be fighting tooth and nail to keep you where you are. Soon you will be seen as a 'remittance man' with nothing to look forward to except early retirement.

— *Fogging* —

Working for a good boss can be the very best kind of management training; working hard for a bad one can be a daily crucifixion, especially if he or she believes that you are plotting to supplant them. Instead of basking in the reflected glory of your excellent performance, the paranoid boss sees every achievement as a threat to his or her security, another nudge down the slope that leads to redundancy. And while some will make it clear that they actively dislike you, others will employ more subtle methods in the hope that you will leave or at least ask to be transferred.

At the centre of such strategies is the desire to frustrate you by enshrouding the key areas of your job in a kind of fog, so that you become progressively more uncertain about what you are supposed to be doing. After all, if you find your objectives confusing, your authority unclear and your immediate priorities downright ambiguous, you are unlikely to turn in as good a performance as you would if such issues were crystal clear. Moreover, by pressing on in the hope that the fog will lift, you risk not only travelling in the wrong direction but of finishing your journey in a multi-car pile-up.

So how can you disperse such a fog? Only by pressing hard for greater clarity. Bombard your boss with *written* requests for a job description and, if he fails to respond, write one yourself and send him a copy. Make sure that it defines your responsibilities, spells out your authority and specifies the resources which you need to do the job. Follow this up with a list of clear-cut objectives, each with a realistic target date. Finally, suggest a few priority tasks to provide a focus for immediate action.

Be sure to keep copies of all these documents and of any replies which you receive. And even if the boss remains silent, do not be discouraged. By taking the initiative you will not only have gained the psychological advantage: in the absence of any feedback you can also feel free to pursue your objectives. After all, you gave him a chance, and he failed to take it. No one will blame you for pressing ahead.

— Rejecting —

Whatever their public protestations, many executives dislike change, since it poses a threat to comfortable routines and may well require them to learn new skills. Those who want to change things face an uphill struggle against the forces of inertia, and are unlikely to win any popularity contests.

It is this natural suspicion of change which enables so many executive deadbeats to pose as 'practical' people who are trying to save the company from power-mad theorists. Those who advocate anything other than the most marginal changes will be castigated as 'phonies' and 'empire builders' who are ignorant of how the business is run. Such charges can be particularly damaging when you are still new to the company. Many may feel that you should be seen but not heard.

How, then, can such critics be silenced? Only by showing that your ideas work, and this means looking for a proving-ground. Fortunately, if you have established good relations with a wide range of executives, there will always be someone who is willing to support you either by supplying you with a problem to work on, or by helping to provide the necessary resources. Given a successful outcome to this 'joint venture' and having made sure that the grapevine is kept well-posted, you can rest assured that other potential clients will beat a path to your door including, hopefully, members of higher management. Out of such small beginnings are reputations built. From now on your critics will be keeping their heads down.

Nevertheless, the surest way of vanquishing the reactionaries is to show those who will be required to operate the new system 'what's in it for them'. If your idea will enable them to earn more money, cut out red tape, make the job safer, eliminate waste, improve quality and, above all, create new customers, then it will have every prospect of being enthusiastically accepted. But you must be prepared to *sell* it and to overcome objections. Those who believe that a good idea 'speaks for itself' show little understanding of human cussedness.

— Victimising —

As a talented person with a burgeoning reputation, you are bound to be envied as well as admired. Whilst most envious people will content themselves with the occasional sneer or 'put-down', others will be more active in seeking your downfall. And while many of their stratagems are easily detected, some will be much more skilfully camouflaged. It is no use looking for a notice marked 'Booby Trap'. The trip wires will be invisible to the naked eye.

Once again, a jealous boss can be a formidable opponent, being obsessed by the thought that you are seeking to topple him. Knowing that you thrive on variety in your work, he will do everything he can to make your life boring by deluging you with time-consuming, mindless chores, most of them simply dreamed up to try to break your spirit. The only way you can break out of this spider's web is to demonstrate how unnecessary all this drudgery is by putting forward ideas which make it redundant. As always, such proposals should be outlined in writing and accompanied by a polite request for an early discussion. Even the most vindictive boss is likely to back off when he recognises that you have placed him in an unwinnable position. For should he persist in his attempts to victimise you, you would have every justification for making a formal complaint. And when the enquiry revealed how he had been treating you, higher management, to put it mildly, would be unlikely to be pleased. Serious questions could be raised about his ability to manage.

Another favourite ploy of the envious superior is to subject you to so-called 'mushroom management': keeping you in the dark as much as possible and, if forced to communicate, feeding you with misleading information. Undoubtedly this can be a most effective stratagem, since to an executive, information is like oxygen: without it he cannot hope to survive. Worse still, since you won't know what you don't know, you are bound to make the occasional embarrassing blunder which can make you appear either inefficient or out of touch. Make no mistake: you cannot afford to continue like this. Unless you take firm action your reputation will soon be in tatters and your hopes of promotion a distant memory.

So what can you do? Quite simply, raise hell. Brush aside those muttered apologies, those insincere 'sorrys' and make it clear that you have had enough. Back up your anger with a typewritten report listing all the incidents and errors which have resulted from your boss' failure to communicate, and make it clear that it is destined for the managing director. Since such bosses are rarely the stuff of which heroes are made, you are likely to receive not only an abject apology, but also a firm promise to pass on in future everything which you need to do your job. While you can scarcely refuse to accept such a commitment, hold on to that report. It is your insurance against any further 'lapses of memory'.

Ambushing

This is a ploy whereby your enemies gang up against you in the hope of sabotaging a new idea which they see as a threat to their status or security. It involves trying to shoot down your idea just after you have presented it, usually in the setting of a formal meeting, a perfectly legitimate vehicle for criticism and discussion. The difference is that the opposition will have been orchestrated before the meeting, and that your critics will arrive with their minds made up. By assailing you with a barrage of hostile comments they hope to influence the uncommitted members and to intimidate the chairman into rejecting your case.

There are three golden rules for handling such verbal mob violence: keep calm, answer courteously and concentrate on driving home your major points. Meet anger with patience, emotion with facts, and show how the company or the department will benefit. Back up your claims with credible statistics, imaginative visuals and the kind of examples to which everyone can relate. Above all, well in advance of the meeting, try to *anticipate* the questions which your critics will be asking: spend some time thinking about their attitudes and concerns. Rest assured that your efforts will be richly rewarded. Not only will your enemies be put to flight, but all those former fence-sitters will rally behind your banner. The chairman's verdict will be a mere formality.

There is no point in refusing to face reality: politics are a part of organisational life, a result of the competition for influence and resources. But politics need not – and indeed are not – simply about squalid power struggles, with the devil taking the innocent or the ill-prepared. Without argument, without persuasion, without the cut-and-thrust of debate and the marshalling of support, an executive's life would be lacking in challenge. Those aiming for the top *need* political skills. Whether we like it or not, we are all salesmen now.

Chapter 13

NEGOTIATING USEFUL ALLIANCES

Learn to make trade-offs – if you have something to sell, someone may want to buy.

Just as in the shifting world of diplomacy, today's enemy can be tomorrow's friend, so it is in business: nothing is forever. Nevertheless, one of the most important of all executive skills – as valid for juniors as for boardroom tycoons – is the ability to negotiate worthwhile alliances which will increase your chances of achieving your goals. While your strategies, once determined, must be rigorously pursued, you can be far more flexible in your choice of tactics. You are like a motorist who, finding one route blocked, is perfectly willing to try another.

Negotiating involves an exchange of satisfactions: there must be something for him as well as something for you. An alliance will last only as long as both parties feel that they are benefitting, and when 'the party's over' it is better to split up amicably. There is no point in engaging in ill-tempered recriminations which will lead inevitably to a noisy separation. The important thing is to know your objectives, and to be clear about what you are willing to concede.

Having the right attitude is the key to success; this is no time to let your heart rule your head. When weighing the merits of a particular strategy, remain clinically detached and examine the evidence. To give way to emotion is to risk losing the game.

The temporary pact

This is the most fleeting kind of alliance, the equivalent of a sexual one-night stand where neither party is looking for a permanent relationship. It is usually sparked by some specific threat to the status quo which would disturb the political balance of power and enable a rival to increase his or her influence.

For example, suppose that you are a plant manager presiding over a large group of people, which consists not only of production personnel but also of the various staff specialists needed to resource them: engineers, accountants, trainers and personnel officers. Imagine that a new director has recently been appointed who sees it as his mission to merge all the service departments into one gigantic 'Administration Group' which naturally he feels should report to him. If such a proposal were to be accepted by the board, you would not only lose control of some valuable resources, you could also be faced by a powerful competitor for the MD's chair. You can hardly stand aside and let *that* happen.

Nevertheless, you would do well to tread warily. To fling yourself into an impetuous all-out assault upon the proposal could easily result in your being dubbed 'a negative thinker' or, more damaging still, a 'blocker': someone who stands in the path of progress. Far better to look around for some potential allies who are likely to share your feelings, for example, your fellow plant managers or the existing heads of engineering and personnel who may feel themselves down-graded by such a restructuring. Having put out some feelers and been warmly received, the next step is to hammer out a common strategy.

Finally, you will need to lobby those directors who are also likely to feel threatened, and who are willing to raise the issue at the next board meeting. Given an objective analysis of the shortcomings of the proposal – showing clearly how it will damage the company – there is no reason why your champions should not be successful. Having achieved its aims, the alliance can then be dissolved. Without a common purpose it would no longer make sense.

Omerta

While mafia 'families' may quarrel among themselves, they have a tradition of remaining silent when confronted by inquisitive outsiders. The same process of closing ranks exists in business. Even the most competitive executives will sometimes unite against a common foe.

The most frequent cause of such atypical behaviour is when a major blunder has occurred in which several executives from different functions are implicated. For example, the failure of a particular sales campaign might be due partly to a poorly-devised consumer research programme and partly to the shortcomings of an inadequately-trained sales force. Assuming that the market research staff report to the Marketing Services Director and the sales force to the Sales Director, then clearly neither senior executive will see much mileage in blaming the other: an enquiry would simply expose his or her own weaknesses. Given such a potentially hazardous situation, it is not surprising that both executives should conclude that those who live in glasshouses shouldn't throw stones and, like experienced mafiosi, parry all attempts to question them.

There are, of course, some types of information-seeker who will always be suspect and who, initially at least, are unlikely to be trusted. Many management consultants fall into this category, particularly those who are carrying out studies of organisation structures or manning levels or – most sinister of all – are attempting to sell the board on the merits of psychological tests. Faced by such threats to the status quo, each executive will see himself in a very real sense as his brother's keeper and will practise various forms of non-cooperation, ranging from non-commital replies to the consultant's questions to a refusal to take part in testing procedures. Given such a display of executive hostility, most boards will show the outsider the door. Clearly the cost of disruption would be far too high.

Sometimes, as frequently happens in multinational companies, the threat arises from within the organisation, usually in the head office of the parent company. Even in the better-managed multinationals, there is a perpetual tension between those in the subsidiary who want to run their own show and those in head office who are seeking to assert their authority. The usual strategy is for the parent to despatch to the subsidiary one or more 'hot-gospellers' for, say, a new marketing planning technique which is confidently expected to usher in the millenium. Needless to say, this is invariably greeted with derision by the seasoned street-fighters of the subsidiary, who regard it as yet further proof of the naïvety and remoteness of 'the folks back home'.

Once again, the threatened executives stand shoulder to shoulder in defusing a potentially dangerous development which, if unchallenged, could rapidly result in further encroachments upon their authority. And again, the same tactics are employed: coolness laced with scepticism, politeness with ambiguity. It is a telling combination and one which invariably sends the 'salesman' scuttling back to head office, convinced that the supposed 'wonder drug' needs further research.

— *Trade-offs* —

Some functions lead cat-and-dog lives, forever squabbling and jealously guarding their respective domains. Production and sales, design and engineering, marketing and accounting: few companies are immune to such internal feuding (hence the emphasis in management training upon 'teambuilding' and 'leadership').

Yet despite such predictable rivalries, shrewd executives know when enough is enough and when compromise is not only sensible but highly desirable. After all, if you cannot hope to win, then at least you should do your best not to lose. A typical example of a situation which often leads to such an impasse is the question of who should control contractors' employees during major plant engineering projects. While local plant management may feel that the responsibility is theirs, the central engineers may take a very different view.

After weeks, perhaps months, of fruitless argument, coupled with much frantic lobbying behind the scenes, it begins to dawn upon both warring factions that neither can hope for an outright victory. Meanwhile, lacking firm direction, the various contractors tend to go their own way, and costs begin to escalate at an alarming rate. Clearly, unless the issue is resolved – and quickly – there can only be one conclusion: head office accountants will begin nosing around and will be quick to point the finger of blame.

Faced by such an horrendous prospect, with all its implications for their future careers, the leaders of both contending groups quickly arrive at a compromise solution, thereby short-circuiting any demand for a head office enquiry. Thus by agreeing to some form of trade-off, both parties emerge with their 'honour' intact and the threat to their careers nipped in the bud. After all, there is no point in persisting in a duel to the death when, even if you win, you are likely to be executed.

Panaceas

Many executives dread their bosses attending outside management courses: all too often they return having learned the wrong lessons. Instead of re-examining their own management style and acquiring knowledge and skills which will make the firm more competitive, some bosses become obsessed with a particular narrow technique which they are convinced will create a kind of New Jerusalem. Invariably such techniques have to do with 'managing people' and are influenced by the latest 'behavioural' theories, however unproven such concepts may be. It can be a testing time for all levels of management since they are expected to make the boss' dream come true by implementing it zealously within their own departments.

Once again, the prudent executive will exercise a little caution.

Instead of rushing in and trumpeting your enthusiasm for the new technique, discuss it thoroughly with some colleagues whose judgment you respect. After all, post-course enthusiasm is a tender vine, and within a few short months the boss may have lost interest. Moreover it is a fact of life that fashions in management development are as volatile as those in pop music: new favourites constantly replace the old. Yet you can scarcely oppose the idea outright while it continues to enjoy the boss' favour. Nor can you simply stand on the sidelines in a sort of apathetic trance.

If, of course, the outcome of your discussions with your colleagues is that the technique is highly relevant and well worth implementing, then there is no problem: you simply go ahead and reap the benefits. But if, as often happens, the consensus is that the idea is useless, if not downright dangerous, then it is vital that you and your colleagues stand together. For if you cannot succeed in persuading your boss during one-to-one discussions, then the only alternative is a coordinated approach, perhaps in the setting of a departmental meeting. Here again, however, it is necessary to devise an agreed strategy either by using a spokesperson who is supported by everyone or by determining beforehand who will raise specific issues.

Such a coordinated approach is not only impressive: it is *effective*. Only the most stubborn – or foolhardy – boss will ignore the opinions of his most experienced lieutenants. Nevertheless, when, in effect, he concedes defeat, let him down lightly by using a diplomatic approach. A suggestion that the matter should be 'reviewed' in three months time will enable him to leave the field with honour. You are unlikely to hear of it ever again.

Poisoned wells

The art of successful negotiating is never to give up more than you are likely to gain, and this requires judgment of the highest order. When considering any proposal, you must think beyond the immediate or short-term benefits, and try to assess the implications for your long-term objectives. It is all too easy to give way to your emotions, and then find that you have walked into a spider's web. And there will be no lack of candidates for the role of spider. For example, as you are more and more recognised as a rising star, you will find yourself cultivated by various fawners and flatterers who will move heaven and earth to ingratiate themselves. Like pilot fish clinging to the mighty shark, they see only profit in such a relationship; for themselves, that is, *not* for you. And indeed they are right, for what could you possibly hope to gain by associating with such people? Were they persons of talent or of shining integrity, theirs would be friendships which would be well worth having, but this, emphatically, is not the case. Mediocre performers and renowned backbiters, they value you only for your ability to protect them and to advance their careers as you climb to the top. And make no mistake: should your career begin to falter, these fair-weather friends would soon melt away. After all, it was not your personality which attracted them in the first place. It was the benefits which you were thought to be capable of delivering.

Social situations can also be tricky. Take, for example, that apparently innocuous invitation to have dinner with a colleague who is by no means one of your closest friends. Is it motivated by a wish to get to know you better, or is it solely to win your support for a scheme which is solely to his advantage? Certainly, you will need to be on your guard until you are satisfied that it is safe to relax, particularly if your wine glass is constantly refilled while your host contents himself with a modest orange juice. And even if you are not directly propositioned, it may be that it is hoped that you will become indiscreet and let slip valuable 'inside information'. If this were to happen and such data were improperly used, it could certainly cause eyebrows to be raised (and questions to be asked) if it became known that *you* were the source of the leak. An executive who cannot keep his or her mouth shut is seen at best as an idiot and at worst as a threat to company security. Few companies will tolerate such a lack of professionalism. Very soon you will find yourself on your way out.

Finally, never put yourself in a position where you can be pressurised, sometimes to an extent which borders upon blackmail. Every organisation has its 'fixers' and 'wheeler-dealers' who can always get you substantial discounts on all kinds of consumer goods and have no difficulty in obtaining those unobtainable tickets. Of one thing you can be certain: such people rarely, if ever, do something for nothing. When they consider the time to be ripe, they will not hesitate to ask you to return the favour, and this could involve you in dubious manoeuvrings from which your integrity may not emerge unscathed. So steer clear of such petty crooks. No discount, however generous, is worth more than your career.

Business is no place for those who long for splendid isolation. Sooner or later, even the loneliest of loners or the most determined individualists are forced to recognise that 'no man is an island' and that some goals can only be achieved by negotiating. The higher you advance in management, the more you recognise the importance of these skills, for without them some obstacles would be virtually impregnable. So learn about negotiating and polish your skills constantly, but don't be upset when you encounter unfairness or even, occasionally, a whiff of sharp practice. Remember: when the stakes are high, ethics may crumble. In business, as in life, you must look out for yourself.

Chapter 14

KEEPING YOUR CAREER MOVING FORWARD

Never rely upon 'career developers' – real high flyers manage their own careers.

However professional their procedures, never rely upon the 'career planners' to advance your career: true high flyers look after themselves. After all, you cannot expect even the most dedicated personnel manager to be constantly brooding over your promotion prospects: it is *your* career and *you* must manage it. While you should certainly consider carefully any genuine opportunities which are offered as part of your 'development plan', these are bound to be a little mechanistic and to lack the flair and creativity which your talents deserve.

If you are to stand out from the crowd, then you must be *opportunistic*: ever alert to seize the kind of opening which could significantly improve your upward mobility. Just as most top jobs are never advertised, so many of the most effective career strategies are rarely discussed in textbooks and seminars, since it is felt that there is something discreditable about them. This, of course, is nonsense; indeed, dangerous nonsense since it encourages the naïve to believe that they need not fend for themselves, as everything will be taken care of by the personnel planners. Shrewd executives are under no such illusion. They see their careers as a business which they alone can manage.

Company-wide assignments

Any opportunity which plucks you from relative obscurity and provides you with a company-wide platform deserves serious consideration. For example, if you were to hear from your boss, or from the grapevine, that a high calibre task force was to be formed to investigate manufacturing costs throughout the company, or to assess the market potential for a new kind of product, you should fight might and main for a place on the team. This kind of assignment is certain to bring you into contact with many influential and up-and-coming people in a wide range of functions and, long after the task has been completed, the relationships (and even, perhaps, the friendships) may endure. This could do you no harm whatever in some future promotion situation, especially the kind where extensive 'soundings' are taken on the merits of the short-listed candidates. The more friends you have who are willing to speak up for you, the better your chances of being selected.

There are, of course, other more technical advantages. In finding out what people think, you invariably find out what they do and, while you cannot hope to become an expert in someone else's function in a matter of days or weeks, you will almost certainly acquire a working knowledge, sufficient for you to be able to 'speak the language'. This will add to your breadth of experience, and enable you to contribute more authoritatively in future to topics which until then had been cloaked in mystery. No longer will you be seen as a narrow specialist.

Equally important is the opportunity which such assignments offer you of understanding how your colleagues in other departments function: the attitudes they bring to their work; the pressures they work under; the issues which tend to dominate their working lives. Once again, such knowledge can be crucial when you are attempting to persuade a particular group to accept a proposal for change. Instead of your being dismissed as 'just another theorist', your presentation will command both interest and respect. Already you will be half-way to 'making a sale'.

— External training courses —

Wounding though it may be to the egos of some management teachers, the technical benefits of most external management courses, in terms of new knowledge and skills, are far exceeded by those free-rein discussions which take place over meals and at the bar. Invariably delegates with similar problems seek each other out and discuss possible solutions. Others exchange views on more general topics, and lace their opinions with real-life case histories from their own companies. A few even succeed in interesting their fellow delegates in their firms' products or services (though this is often regarded as being rather 'pushy'). The longer the course lasts, the more likely it is that such relationships will put down roots, far beyond the mere exchange of business cards.

Again, you should regard such contacts as a long-term investment rather than as something which is likely to pay off immediately. For if you are patient and nurture the relationship carefully (the occasional note or phone call, the exchange of cards at Christmas), there are plenty of potential benefits to be reaped. Firstly, such contacts give you a window on the outside world: a means of keeping in touch with what other companies are doing. Secondly, they provide you with a number of people with whom you can exchange ideas, and from whom you can expect to receive objective advice. Thirdly, given a relationship where there is a growing respect for each other's abilities, it is highly probable that your name will be mentioned in all kinds of business situations – many of them of a social nature – which will help to build up your reputation in your field. And while you may be happy in your job and perfectly content with your present company, it ought not to displease you if your name is noted by headhunters. Things can change quickly, and not always for the better.

Hotly though some companies may deny it, your performance on the course itself can also influence your career prospects, especially if the programme is focussed upon general management issues rather than upon specialist skills. While the course tutors may not be required to submit a formal report to your boss on how well you performed, it is by no means uncommon – especially in the case of in-company courses – for bosses and senior personnel planners to ask the tutors what they thought of you. And while no doubt they will strive to be as objective as possible, the tutors would be less than human if they did not tend to comment more favourably upon a delegate who was always 'positive' in his contributions rather than one who was grumpy or cynical or appeared to 'know it all'.

Without in any way behaving like a sycophant, there is nothing to be gained and, potentially, much to be lost by acquiring a reputation as a 'difficult' course delegate. The stronger your personality and the keener your brain, the more you must resist the temptation to run rings around the faculty, egged on by your admirers among the delegates. Don't risk a quite unnecessary black mark on your record through your eagerness to win a little short-term 'glory'. Control your ego, keep a check on your emotions and take every opportunity to increase your knowledge and skill.

Presentations at conferences

If you work for a company which is famous for its success in a key aspect of business such as marketing or finance, you may find yourself receiving invitations to speak at external management conferences. Since most progressive firms look upon such occasions as gilt-edged public relations opportunities, you will be encouraged, indeed expected, to accept these invitations and to acquit yourself well. This is yet another reason why you should strive to become an accomplished public speaker. The better your presentations, the greater your prestige: the greater your prestige, the better your prospects of early advancement.

Nevertheless, it is not only external conferences which deserve your attention. Many large companies hold both annual management conferences (which are often reserved for the firm's most senior executives) and divisional conferences which are usually centred around the various sales forces. Both types of conference offer up-and-coming executives excellent opportunities to sell their ideas, project their personalities, lobby for support and generally make a resounding impact. And, once again, your behaviour off the platform can be just as important as the presentation itself. Even though you may not particularly enjoy drinking, time spent at the bar can be time well spent. Moreover, there is no need to worry about exceeding your limit. One gin and tonic, topped up with tonic, will keep you convivial and sober for the whole of the evening.

However well known you become in your field, never be too proud to attend these divisional conferences. Just as an MP must visit his constituency regularly in order to maintain his popularity, so, too, must you build up your 'fan club' by never being too busy to give a well thought-out speech. Once you are respected throughout an organisation, you are more than half-way to being promoted. It is not just a matter of who you know. It can also be a matter of by whom you are known.

— *Improving your qualifications* —

Assuming that you already have a first degree or an equivalent qualification, is there any further need to add to your academic honours, or should you concentrate instead upon widening your experience? The answer is that you should strive to do both, for in today's competitive business world anything which will give you an 'edge' over your rivals is well worth pursuing. And the most valuable 'edge' of all is to have an MBA.

It is not so much the degree itself that is important: it is what it says about you, particularly about your commitment to a business career. No one who is lacking in dedication is going to submit himself or herself to a rigorous schedule of lectures, case studies and projects which require not only intellectual stamina but heroic qualities of determination and will power. If you can persuade your firm to fund you for a year as a full-time MBA student, then at least you will be able to concentrate your energies. If not, then you should consider undertaking a 'distance learning programme' (now offered by a number of business schools) which will enable you to study at home over a longer period. Your company training manager will have the details, and the company may also be willing to help with books and fees.

Accountancy qualifications are also well worth obtaining, especially now that the profession is no longer dominated by 'abominable no men' and penny-pinchers who could be relied upon to stamp on promising new ideas. Today's accountant is a much broader individual than his predecessor, and is usually a respected member of the business team to which he is attached (the days of gigantic centralised accounting departments are virtually over). Another extremely useful qualification is a degree or diploma in information technology or computer studies. The current explosion in IT throughout business is unlikely to abate in the foreseeable future, and the outlook for any executive who remains unfamiliar with these new tools will be bleak indeed.

Finally, it goes without saying that if you intend to pursue a career in a staff role, be it personnel, procurement or management development, then it is well worth studying for whatever is perceived as the most prestigious qualification in your field. Again this will be seen as evidence of professionalism and commitment and, in the relatively near future, those lacking such qualifications are unlikely to attain senior posts.

Strategic socialising

There are many events in business which can provide opportunities for you to widen your circle of contacts. For example, such familiar rituals as retirement parties and long-service award presentations, annual outings and office Christmas parties can all enable you to meet new people, not least those in senior positions who you may be keen to impress. While a few senior executives are extremely status-conscious and unwilling to fraternise with those of lower rank, the majority are happy to socialise quite freely, believing that by doing so they remain 'in touch'.

The most important point to remember on such occasions is that most senior people will have come to enjoy themselves, and will resent being ambushed into a serious discussion about work. Far better to keep the conversation soufflé-light by confining it to such perennially 'safe' topics as sport, holidays and, best of all, the executive himself. Most senior male executives are only too willing to talk about themselves and their experiences, or to reminisce about 'the good old days' when they first joined the company. Once you have got them launched on some favourite topic, you need not worry about your own contributions: your job is to listen and to *show* that you are listening. An attentive air and a nodding head will make a far greater impact than any number of 'sophisticated' witticisms, which may only convince the speaker that you are trying to upstage him. Yours is decidedly a supporting role, but if you play it skilfully you will make a most agreeable first impression.

Mingling with the delegates at outside management conferences, and even more so with the speakers, is another valuable source of contacts, some of whom could prove useful in the future. The same applies to the branch meetings of professional associations and to those of nationwide management organisations. While the speakers may not always be inspiring, they invariably know their subjects, and are usually generous with their time in answering questions. By attending such meetings you can sometimes come away with a solution to a problem which has been troubling you, as well as adding to your network of contacts.

— *Developing subordinates* —

However dedicated you may be to achieving your own career goals, never neglect to develop your subordinates. Not only does a high-performing group reflect credit upon you, the boss, it also enhances your promotion prospects. The point to remember about any promotion situation is that, if you are successful, your own job will become vacant. Why not, therefore, make it easier for the selectors to fill your post by carefully developing a high-calibre successor who is capable of taking over right away, thus sparing the selectors yet another problem? Make no mistake: in a closely-fought contest for a promotion vacancy, it is factors such as these which can give you a much-needed 'edge' over the other candidates. This is one of the many reasons why delegation is such a vital management skill. By developing others you develop yourself.

It is, of course, vital that your efforts do not go unnoticed, or you may not reap the benefits which are rightly yours. Make sure that you keep your boss fully informed on your plans for developing your high flyers, and give him regular feedback on their performance. Above all, let him see their progress for himself by inviting him to meetings to hear their presentations and to observe how they present and defend their ideas. Not only will your own reports be confirmed, but your boss is likely to feel much more relaxed about the prospect of losing you when your name comes up as a promotion candidate.

If you want to be a successful business manager, you must be willing and able to manage yourself. The moment when you feel that you can sit back and let others provide you with development opportunities is the moment when your career will begin to stagnate. Faced with ever-increasing competition for a diminishing supply of management jobs, only the fittest and the sharpest will make it to the top. So develop yourself *and keep on developing*. The truth of it is: you don't have a choice.

Chapter 15

PROFITING FROM PANICS

Welcome a crisis – there's no better opportunity for you to prove your worth.

Anyone seeking a quiet life should forget about a career in business: stress and pressure are part of the job. Nor should the would-be tycoon take too much comfort from those management text books where all executives are 'effective' and all managers are 'rational'. The truth is that there is nothing like a good, old-fashioned 'panic' to sort the winners from the losers, the promotable from the disposable. Far from fearing the occasional crisis, you should welcome it with open arms. It gives you a splendid opportunity to show what you are made of.

Being able to function effectively in a crisis is a question of retaining your sense of proportion while all those around you are losing theirs. Indeed the very atmosphere of a panic-stricken organisation with its communications catastrophes and bewildered employees, its rampant grapevine and paralysed leadership, is a perfect setting for a potent injection of ice-cold analysis and decisive action. Yet if there is one quality above all which you will need in order to survive, it is, without question, a sense of humour. Without it every molehill can seem like a mountain and every setback a crushing defeat.

To survive, let alone profit from a panic, you need to be flexible: a fleet-footed stallion rather than a lumbering dinosaur. While others cling to outdated policies and traditional thinking, look for an approach which exposes the *cause* of the problem, not simply its effects.

— Storm signals —

Some kinds of crisis are totally foreseeable: others explode like thunderclaps out of a clear blue sky. The easiest kind of panic to forecast is when some longstanding inefficiency finally reaps its grim reward. Take the all-too-familiar example of the major customer who, after months of complaining about poor quality, late deliveries or indifferent servicing, threatens to take his business elsewhere: an outcome as predictable as night following day. Nevertheless, predictable or not, it presents you with an opportunity to retrieve the situation by putting forward a strategy for restoring customer goodwill. Needless to say, this should not be the kind of proposal which, to be effective, would require a series of miracles: however radical its ideas, it should be perfectly feasible. This means, of course, that it must make sense in terms of costs and existing resources: saving the account should not spell ruin for the company. Such plans, then, must be carefully prepared, the fruit of much painstaking investigation. Whereas previously your ideas may have been considered fanciful, with disaster looming they will command attention.

Even so, it is possible to fumble the opportunity through poor presentation and, above all, bad psychology. Remember that the people who you will be attempting to convince will almost certainly include those who are responsible for the current crisis. At a time when they are probably feeling somewhat guilty and insecure – and therefore aggressive – there is nothing to be gained by seeming to present yourself as an avenging angel who has been sent to put the incompetent to flight. For whatever you may feel about your colleagues' shortcomings, you will need their cooperation in implementing your plan. And if they feel humiliated, you are unlikely to receive it.

Even many so-called 'acts of God' – crises which, it is claimed, no one could have predicted – are not always as capricious as they may at first seem. Wherever there is a significant weakness in an organisation, be it in its products, policies or procedures, there you will find the seed-bed of a future crisis. And while you may have pointed out the weakness on many occasions – and put forward some ideas for dealing with it – nothing may have been done. But do not be discouraged: your time has now come. Once the problem has blossomed into a full-scale 'panic' there will be listeners a-plenty for what you propose and it will appear to many that you have saved the day. All that frustration will have been well worthwhile. You will be well on your way to becoming a company 'star'.

Recessional behaviour

Sooner or later every company enters a period of recession when sales fall, unit costs rise and those brave-new-world projects are put into cold storage. The more prosperous a company has been in the past, the more traumatic the impact of its current misfortunes. As share prices fall and stock options begin to suffer, frowns replace smiles in the corridors of power and as the spectre of redundancy looms ever closer, some executives start thinking of 'jumping ship'.

Yet, for the ambitious executive, this is a time of opportunity, not a time for losing heart. While lesser men update their CVs or study the appointments columns of the quality newspapers, *you* make your mark with some decisive action. First, you show that you understand economic realities by launching an all-out attack upon non-essential expenditure. Postpone sales conferences, vet expense accounts rigorously and issue new and stricter guidelines on client entertainment. Moreover, when staff leave the company, resist the temptation to replace them immediately; instead, look upon such vacancies as an opportunity both to re-organise jobs and to redeploy people. Far from resenting such moves, most of your staff will positively welcome them, especially those who are anxious to widen their experience. With fresh ideas and a new vigour blowing through your department, morale will once again begin to rise. It is boredom and lack of challenge that kill enthusiasm.

Naturally, during such a stressful period, your communications with your group must be immaculate. It is at times like these that the grapevine can run wild and cause credence to be given to even the most ludicrous rumours. Make sure that your immediate subordinates are kept well-briefed on all important developments, and that they pass on the news to their own subordinates. If and when some critical event occurs, or if some particularly wild rumour is sweeping the company, call a meeting of your total group and set out the facts as you believe them to be (having checked them, if necessary, with your boss or Personnel). Encourage questions and answer them frankly. There is nothing to be gained by 'conning' people, and your candid approach will be greatly appreciated. It is fear of the unknown which undermines morale and performance.

Needless to say, during a recession, your behaviour and performance will come under scrutiny both from above and below. Your boss will appreciate your cost-cutting measures, especially when they have been taken on your own initiative. Your subordinates, too, are likely to be reassured by your positive leadership. But be warned: as long as the crisis lasts, you must be willing to live by your own precepts. Many a 'let's all pull together' atmosphere has been soured by a few thoughtless actions. For example, a boss who exhorts his subordinates to cut down on business lunches while continuing to entertain lavishly himself will rapidly lose his credibility as a leader. When belts have been tightened, yours must not be the first to slacken.

Counter-punching

The more serious the crisis, the greater the opportunity for you to sell your ideas. After all, the very fact that the company is in a mess is a sure indication that there is plenty of scope for improvement. Like a decimated forest in the aftermath of a hurricane, many traditional strategies and methods will have come crashing down, creating space for imaginative new thinking. In more prosperous times it might have been difficult to get a hearing. Now complacency is in full retreat.

There is no mystery about the kind of ideas which are going to be listened to: those which claim to make or save money. But, remember, this is a crisis, not a minor hiccup, and your idea, if accepted, must start to pay off immediately. This is no time to present that dazzling new long-term marketing strategy which could be the company's salvation, but which would need at least three years before it produced any benefits. After all, unless the company manages to stay afloat during the present storm, talk of a long-term future may seem distinctly academic.

Assuming, however, that the idea is realistic and feasible, punch home its advantages as hard as you can. Take heart from the fact that, no matter how radical your approach, the 'law of the situation' will be very much on your side. Your opponents, if any, will represent the discredited past while you, by contrast, are the hope of the future. Nonetheless, despite having such a resounding psychological advantage, take care that your presentation is thoroughly professional. Clear-cut objectives, attractive benefits and a believable strategy for implementation: these are the three pillars of an effective presentation. Make sure that you don't fall at the first fence.

Once the firm has survived the worst of the storm and calmer conditions are beginning to return, you can start to produce some of your more long-term ideas which could involve any number of major changes. Depending upon what the priorities are in your organisation's marketplace, *now* is the time to unfold your plans for, say, a major updating of the firm's technologies, an R&D drive to develop new products, or the closing down of unprofitable operations. If you wait until things have returned to 'normal', you risk encountering your old enemy, complacency. *Strike while your fame is still at its height*. Remember: if your plans are accepted, they will *have* to promote you. You are the only one who can be relied upon to carry them through.

— Guiding, wining and dining —

Many executives are thrown into a panic by VIP visitors, seeing them at best as an irritation and at worst as a threat. True, such visits can be extremely time-consuming, requiring as they do meticulous planning and preparation, yet without a doubt they offer an ambitious high flyer an excellent opportunity to add to his or her laurels. Once again, such fleeting contacts may turn up trumps in the future, since your name may be remembered at vital moments when discussions are being held about promotion vacancies. This is especially true of those US multinationals which believe in regular visits to their overseas subsidiaries. To have impressed a powerful vice-president during a two-day visit can sometimes help your career more than many years of hard slog.

The secret of a successful visit is to find out what your visitors would like to see or hear about, and then plan the programme to meet these objectives. Obvious though it may seem, this is often ignored by flustered executives who provide a 'menu' which is convenient for them, but which may have little attraction for a particular visitor. Some senior executives resent having to plod around the same old factories or, worse still, having to sit in a conference room listening to endless presentations. They will appreciate a schedule which gives them what *they* want, and which shows every sign of having been carefully tailored.

Many VIPs dislike too regimented a programme, one which provides little scope for ad hoc discussions or unscheduled visits to particular areas. They are well aware of the artificiality which surrounds their visit – the unnaturally tidy work areas, the over-polished presentations, the carefully-selected speakers – and would often much rather make up their minds for themselves. For you, the organising executive, this means letting your visitor 'breathe' by allowing him to spend at least a part of his time 'doing his own thing'. Some executives are horrified at the thought of their VIP visitor moving around the company without an accompanying phalanx of executives and – horror of horrors – conversing democratically with the workers and staff. Yet this is exactly the kind of freedom which the more discerning VIPs relish, and no amount of showbiz gloss in the formal programme can match the satisfaction which they get from finding things out for themselves. Remember, such people are accustomed to a high degree of stage management during their visits, and become rather bored by it. A fresh approach, with greater freedom and spontaneity, is far more likely to be appreciated – and remembered.

Finally, it can often be a mistake to bundle your guest into a five-star restaurant for a heavy lunch when he or she would probably much rather have a salad in the company canteen. American executives, in particular, like to have a chance to chat with new people, and are unlikely to be concerned at the absence of gourmet food. They are far more interested in finding out what really goes on.

Media moments

Getting unfavourable publicity in the national press or on TV is a nightmare which haunts many organisations, and when it occurs, it can strike terror into the stoutest hearts. All kinds of incidents can trigger off a furore, and it is often the most commonplace which generate the worst publicity. A few ill-chosen words from a supervisor which result in a walk-out; the dismissal of a female employee (especially if she is pregnant or looks after her aged mother): these are the kind of 'human interest' stories which get into the newspapers and cause executives to be interrogated as though they were on trial.

Given the increasing interest of the media in business and its insatiable appetite for exposing possible 'cover-ups', it is by no means a waste of time for rising executives to learn how to handle investigative reporters. All too often, a company which is the object of media attention is like a beleagured fortress. Staff are forbidden to talk to the press; meetings are cancelled and conferences postponed, and top managers huddle in their elegant offices, praying that the storm will soon blow over. As a result of such negative policies, the public becomes convinced that the company is hiding something and 'rent a crowd' troublemakers have a field day. And when at last the firm moves to defend itself it is often too late. The corporate image has been severely dented.

Should you find yourself being interviewed by the media, look upon it not as an ordeal, but as an opportunity to make your mark. But keep in mind three things. First, the reporter is likely to be highly suspicious of anything which smacks of PR double-talk. If blatant errors have been made, don't try to cover them up: *say what is being done to stop them happening again*. Second, reporters are not coroners: they are in the *entertainment business*. If they sometimes appear less concerned with factual detail than with attitudes, less with deeds than with underlying motives, it is because these are the things which interest their readers/viewers. Lastly, no matter how much you may be needled by the interviewer, don't take it personally. Keep your emotions under control and your answers brief and to the point.

Being able to deal effectively with the media is an increasingly sought-after executive skill. Should you be given the opportunity of being trained in how to cope with TV and radio interviews, grasp it with both hands. It could benefit both your company and your future career.

There is, of course, a whole battery of smaller-scale panics which, though relatively minor, can sometimes be embarrassing: the early morning fog which causes you to miss your plane; the projector which fails during a boardroom presentation; the missing file which the boss needs in five minutes flat; the guest speaker who arrives in a tipsy condition. But this is what business is all about: a roller-coaster world of triumph and setback. And yet would you *really* have it any other way? Those whom the gods would promote they first test with a crisis.

Chapter 16

IMPRESSING TOP PEOPLE

Do what the expert yachtsman does – trim your sails to the prevailing wind.

Getting to the top in business requires many of the skills of the expert yachtsman. Just as the sailor needs to trim his sails to the prevailing wind, so the ambitious executive must be ever alert to changes in the corporate power game, to the ebb and flow of top management fortunes. For it is here at the apex of the management pyramid where risk and reward are uneasy bedfellows that those impressions are made which can shape your career. And if you falter badly, there may be no second chance.

— *Aiming for excellence* —

In today's competitive climate the only way to stake your claim to a seat at the summit is to perform superbly; neither bluff nor influence are adequate substitutes. But to forge a reputation that causes your name to be remembered requires not only talent and outstanding dedication; it calls for an ability to detect those assignments where success is most likely to be widely publicised, and hence to catch the attention of the Great Ones upstairs.

Don't waste your time on worthy yet essentially boring activities which are unlikely to arouse a flicker of interest at the upper echelons. Keep burying yourself in 'working parties', and you may well end up by burying your career. Instead, concentrate your efforts on those tasks where success will really make a difference to the firm's ability to achieve its business goals. Any activity which wins new and important customers, improves the quality of the product or service, gives the firm a technological 'edge' or attracts favourable publicity (especially on TV) is virtually certain to put your name in lights and cause your personnel file to be sent for by the managing director.

Yet it is precisely at such moments of triumph that you must keep your head, or risk making enemies who could damage your career. Even though you may have been publicly commended by the MD and had your photograph splashed across the front page of the company newspaper, you must appear to be untouched by your sudden fame, and seem reluctant to step into the spotlight's glare. Accept all trophies on behalf of your 'team', stress the contribution made by 'colleagues' in other departments, and appear mildly embarrassed by all the acclaim (for which, nonetheless, you are 'deeply grateful'). Such modesty will calm even the most envious onlookers and will remove the sting from your competitors' defeat. Even their congratulations may begin to sound sincere.

Cosseting the customer

Until a few years ago, the front-running cliché in the typical annual report – one endlessly repeated at management conferences – was that champion toe-curler 'people are our greatest asset'. In the cut-and-thrust of today's market economies, this venerable old nag has been put out to graze, and has been succeeded by a fleet-footed young stallion who has captured the hearts of chairmen everywhere: his name, of course, is Customer Care. Here at last is the winner of winners, the standard around which all can rally, the juju which wards off evil spirits, the mantra which invokes divine support.

Now in business one should never look the proverbial gift horse in the mouth. If customer care is the 'flavour of the decade', as assuredly it deserves to be, then bend your every effort to demonstrating that you are a true believer. For despite the reproaches of the behavioural scientists, people still run a very poor third behind profitability and growth in the overwhelming majority of business organisations. The slogan 'People First', so proudly flaunted when times are good, is soon transformed into 'People Suffer First' when times are bad. Verily, by their redundancies ye shall know them.

Any activity which is manifestly designed to create new customers and to increase the satisfactions of existing ones is a sure-fire route to executive stardom. Dealing promptly and vigorously with customer complaints, visiting key accounts regularly to check on new or emerging needs, providing customers with first-class back-up services including, where necessary, training: these are the kind of activities which build customer loyalty (and prompt congratulatory letters to a delighted chairman).

While sales executives are perhaps best placed to establish close relationships with customers, there is still plenty of scope for contributors from other functions. Technical advice, accounting and purchasing expertise, training courses offered at knock-down fees: these are just some of the 'golden handcuffs' which can bind customers to firms which appear to care. The message for any thrusting executive is clear: review your objectives and give top priority to those which will most benefit the customer. These are the ones where the rewards of success are most speedily harvested.

Spreading the word

More than at any other time in history, this is the Age of the Conference. Like lemmings gathering for a last leap into the unknown, executives constantly congregate in five-star hotels, ever searching for that Holy Grail which will enable them to survive in an uncertain world. From America and Japan, and with occasional stragglers from Europe, hundreds of gurus mount spotlighted podiums to feed those earnest seekers-after-truth who can afford their fees. Cursed are the poor for they shall be disappointed.

But take heart: you do not *have* to be a guru to claim a share of this particular kingdom. Albeit at a slightly less glamorous level, there are plenty of opportunities to act as an ambassador for your company, and to present its products and services in the best possible light. Institutes of management, professional associations, chambers of commerce, Rotary Clubs and Round Tables; these are just a few of the many organisations which are constantly seeking company speakers, especially if the firm is reasonably well-known or manufactures products with household names. Then there are those 'seminars' and 'workshops' which like to feature speakers with 'hands on' experience of a particular technique: a strategy which may sometimes exclude academics but which most certainly includes practising executives.

It is these more modest opportunities that you should snap up whenever they are offered, having first obtained your company's approval. After all, even though they may lack the glamour of the more prestigious conference, they nevertheless offer a two-fold public relations opportunity: to build the reputation of your firm in the market place, and to get your name known in your particular field. Provided that you are ready to learn the tricks of the speaker's trade – how to prepare a presentation and deliver it competently – you will soon be regarded by your company as a valuable spokesman who can be relied upon to generate public goodwill.

Perhaps the most prestigious kind of speaking engagement is when you are invited to present a real-life case history covering a business activity for which your company is especially renowned. If, for example, the firm is revered for its spectacular track record in developing new products, or is an acknowledged innovator in marketing strategy, then you can quickly build up the sort of reputation which makes you an automatic choice on that particular subject. However, as always, the price of such success is that it can easily irritate envious colleagues, and soon there may be mutterings about the amount of time that you are spending away from the office (together with much overheated speculation about the size of your fees). The only way to combat such jealousy is to take nothing for granted, to seek higher management's approval before you accept *any* invitation and, above all, to pay any fees which you receive into the company's coffers. This may seem a somewhat spartan doctrine, but there is really no alternative if you wish to silence those wagging tongues. By forgoing the occasional modest fee, you will preserve your image as a 'Mr Clean' whose loyalty to the company always comes first.

Working in the community

Ever sensitive to their public image, companies are always anxious to represent themselves as 'good corporate citizens' who enrich the lives of the communities which they serve. And make no mistake, there are many kinds of activities where there is a ready market for executives' talents: as fund-raisers for local charities, as school governors, as treasurers of church councils, as organisers of fêtes and bazaars for worthy causes. Once again, apart from the intrinsic satisfaction of helping the weak and underprivileged, there is another notable benefit in becoming a local 'celebrity': it reflects well upon your employer as well as upon yourself.

This can be a particularly valuable asset when your company is a major employer in the area, but has to compete for labour with several other organisations. The better the firm's reputation, the more likely it is that it will attract the best of the available local talent, for it is far more likely to be judged by the kind of people who work for it than by its glossy recruitment brochures. A company which encourages its employees to join in community activities and to accept leadership roles will have an edge over one which prefers to stand aloof. The lesson is clear: get involved, take responsibility and put your talents to work on worthwhile projects. The company will be happy to bask in your reflected glory, and will not be unmindful of where the credit lies.

There are, however, one or two caveats which any high-flying executive ought to observe. The most important one is to avoid too close an involvement with local politics. Gone are the days when companies were largely managed by right-wing zealots with hard-line views on a myriad of social issues. Today a much wider range of opinions is tolerated and, perhaps surprisingly, some of the more 'progressive' political views are to be found in or near the boardroom. There is absolutely no point in arousing latent political hostility by nailing your own colours too firmly to the mast, thereby handing your competitors a potential advantage. Remember, too, that firms have to do business with all kinds of governments and all kinds of councils, and that too partisan a stance on political matters can sometimes result in orders being lost and contracts awarded to less strident competitors. So leave politics to the politicians. An executive should stick to what he does best.

Social occasions

Hob-nobbing with top management at cocktail parties and formal dinners can provide a searching test of your social skills, for it is here that you will meet people who can either accelerate your progress or – if they dislike you – poison your well. Make no mistake: here are men and women with well-developed egos who are often convinced that they can spot future 'winners' on the basis of a few minutes' casual chat. Not for them the subtleties of psychological tests. A fellow's handshake can be far more revealing.

Nevertheless, you need not approach such occasions in a state of high tension, for there are three golden rules which are easy to follow. First, never take the initiative when conversing with a Great One: selecting the topic is a privilege of rank. After all, if you attempt to lead when you ought to be following, you could be inviting the kind of social disaster which could snuff out your career in a matter of minutes. Suppose, for example, that you try to start a conversation on classical music only to be told by the Great One that it bores him stiff. Or – assuming that all top managers are fanatical golfers – you enquire as to his handicap only to be rebuffed with 'I never play'. It is pointless to run such unnecessary risks. Yours is to react, not to direct.

The second great rule follows on from the first: cultivate the skills of *active listening*. Forget all those brilliant epigrams and in-depth analyses, and just keep reinforcing his conviction that he is a sparkling raconteur. How can you do this? Simply by leaning forward slightly, maintaining plenty of eye contact and throwing in the occasional 'uh-huh' if he begins to falter. If he is the strong, taciturn type, smile encouragingly and keep nodding vigorously at 30-second intervals. Above all, concentrate as though your life depended upon it for you cannot afford to be caught napping should he ask you a question. Given such an attentive listener, the Great One's self-esteem will rise to unprecedented heights, and he will be grateful to you for making him feel so good. By restraining your ego you will have made a friend for life.

Finally, be careful about using humour. A story which may convulse one person may leave another stony-faced, and it may not be worth the risk of striking the wrong note. Only if you know the Great One well, and understand his sense of humour should you attempt to amuse him, for it can be truly demoralising if a joke falls flat. Once again, it is far better to play it safe and to react to your partner's quips, however feeble, as though you were in the presence of a second Oscar Wilde. After all, no one ever got fired through laughing in the right place. It is the would-be court jester who risks losing the king's favour.

Entertaining

If you work for a big multinational, or at a location which is some distance from head office, you may find yourself occasionally having to entertain a visiting VIP. This is a situation which can have many tense moments for there is not only the fundamental issue of whether you have much in common with each other, but also whether you can provide the kind of entertainment which your guest prefers. It can be disastrous, for example, to bundle your VIP into a famous steak house, only to find that he is a vegetarian, or to assume that, like you, he will enjoy Chinese cuisine. Worse still, whatever his gastronomic preferences happen to be, you may catch him at a time when he is trying to lose weight. Rather than run the risk of horrendous last-minute embarrassment, ask him what kind of food he prefers *before* planning the evening or – if you would find that too intimidating – telephone his secretary who will usually be only too pleased to help you.

The same principle of 'ask before you book' is equally valid when the question arises of obtaining tickets for a theatre or concert. There is no point in moving heaven and earth to get tickets for 'the hottest show in town' only to find that he loathes that kind of play. Nor should you plan the evening on the basis of any preconceived notions of national preferences. Not every Italian will thank you for a seat at Covent Garden, nor will every American enthuse over the latest musical. Japanese executives, in particular, often find the Western sense of humour difficult to appreciate, and should be kept well away from the kind of high-speed bedroom farce that may well delight a Frenchman.

Perhaps the best kind of entertainment, provided that you can avoid the pitfalls, is to invite your guest to dinner in your own home: Americans, in particular, will appreciate a more personalised approach. It is a fallacy to suppose that all foreign visitors are panting for exotic dishes, fashionable restaurants and challenging cultural experiences. They tend to be far more relaxed in a cosy room in a pleasant home where they can join in the normal life of the family: meet your wife and children, look at some family photographs, pat the dog and take off their jackets if they feel too warm. The key question, of course, is whether your partner is comfortable with the idea of entertaining at home; if not, forget it. Domestic undercurrents are not difficult to detect, and you do not want it to be thought that you have marriage problems.

Finally, remember that impressing top management should be a low-key operation, not a raucous exercise in self-promotion. Keep a low profile, let others sing your praises, and talk about the job, never yourself. Such humility may seem strange to those thrusting executives who wear their 'assertiveness' like a second skin. But life in business is not all struggle. Sometimes the meek inherit the earth.

Part IV

Power is the Prize

O Captain! my captain! our fearful
trip is done,
The ship has weather'd every rack
the prize we sought is won.

Walt Whitman, O Captain! My Captain!

Chapter 17

TAKING CHARGE

Share your hopes and plans for the future – people won't expect miracles but they'll respond to a vision.

It's not a dream: it's happened. You have run your last lap, holed your last putt and clambered in triumph to the topmost peak. You are no longer the instrument of other people's strategies. You are a giver of instructions, a maker of choices, a tribal deity who commands respect. No longer need you dance to other men's tunes. You are the chief executive. You can write your own music.

Yet power is a heady wine: one which should be sipped, not flung back like vodka. Unless the company is trembling on the brink of bankruptcy or fighting for its life against a determined predator, it is better to spend some time initially in perfecting that long-term strategy to which every major decision must in future contribute. Such strategising is vital, since, without specific long-term goals, it is all too easy to become immersed in a morass of trivialities which have nothing to do with what your job is about: thinking about the future and providing leadership.

— The Grand Tour —

If you work for a large organisation, especially one which is fragmented among numerous locations, it is virtually certain that many employees will not have the faintest idea who you are or what you look like. All they know is that there is a new boss at head office, but they could pass you in the street without a flicker of recognition. It is no use deploring their lack of company-consciousness. It is up to *you* to go out and make yourself known.

Start with your home territory: head office itself. Here you have a choice between addressing a number of large-ish meetings, consisting of various groups of employees (executives, middle managers, administrative staff) or going for a more informal, low-key approach by making unscheduled appearances in the various departments. The advantage of the large meeting is that you can communicate your key messages in an organised fashion, and also deal with any issues which may be worrying people, such as rumours about redundancies or takeover bids. It is also a time-efficient way of meeting large numbers of employees.

Nevertheless, not even the best-run meeting can match the much greater impact of the whistle-stop tour of each department, chatting to employees, shaking hands, asking friendly questions about an individual's job or length of service, and listening attentively to the replies. And smiling, always smiling. True, you cannot hope to talk to every person you meet, but that doesn't matter. You can count upon the people you chat with to give a detailed report to their colleagues, probably couched in the most glowing terms.

Don't neglect the 'corporate outposts': those regional offices and distant factories where visits from senior head office executives are as rare as golden eagles in suburban London. If you want every part of the company to pull together, remember that you are ideally placed to be the unifying force, and this means that you must be *seen* if your words are to be believed. Remember, too, that those parts of the company which work shifts offer particularly rewarding public relations opportunities. Pictures in the company newspaper showing the chief executive in earnest discussion with members of the night shift can help to project the image of a strong, purposeful, no-nonsense leader who 'knows how the other half lives'.

Keep your eyes and ears open during your visit. Encourage people to speak their minds and don't be hurt if they take you at your word.

— Attending conferences —

In-company conferences can provide you with many opportunities to meet new people and to re-establish contact with others who you may know slightly, but not at all well. You can either take an active part in the conference – giving a keynote speech or joining in some of the discussions – or content yourself with a more passive role in which you contribute little except your personal charm. Either way, whether you actively participate or keep your own counsel, you will be seen by those whose leader you are, and such judgements as are made of you are likely to be positive. You cannot inspire confidence, still less loyalty, if you are perceived as a kind of executive Trappist who rarely ventures outside his office.

Going to conferences also gives you a splendid opportunity to see some of the participating executives in action and to evaluate their capabilities at first-hand. There are many valuable sources of information which can be tapped; some formal, others less structured. For example, an executive's ability to deliver a convincing presentation can tell you a good deal about his ability to construct a logical argument, and whether he can infect others with his own enthusiasm. Then again, his ability to chair the conference effectively, or to keep a lively group discussion on track, can reveal whether he can assert himself without giving offence to people with strong convictions. Leadership, after all, is not about whether a person possesses a magical set of personality traits, but whether he can get the required results in the available time. A crowded conference agenda provides as good a test as any.

However, it is not only the conference set-pieces that can help you to assess the potential of your new subordinates: social occasions can be equally rewarding. Is the executive a good mixer, moving easily from group to group, or does he circulate only among a few obvious cronies? Does he *listen* to other people and ask them questions, or does he seem to want to dominate every discussion? Can he hold his liquor, or does he become dangerously indiscreet after even a short time at the bar? Are people likely to respect him and be willing to follow him? Would *you* be happy to do so if he were in *your* job?

One final point. Watch out for those self-promoting opportunists who are invariably to be found at any company conference, though mercifully in very small numbers. These are the axe-grinders, the ear-benders, the smooth-talking fixers who see you as someone to be 'conned' into believing that they are better than they are. Unhappily, not a few supposedly mature and experienced chief executives have succumbed to the wiles of these specious wordsmiths, only to discover that promise and performance can be worlds apart. Should you be impressed by some plausible character whose background and experience seem to be quite exceptional, check his track record when you return to the office. It may well be that he is all that he seems to be, in which case you have a name for your 'people to watch' list. But it could also transpire that he is a man of straw who lacks the ability to convert ideas into action, and whose determination evaporates when the going gets rough.

— Management meetings —

Your first few Board meetings can be crucial in establishing your credibility with your senior colleagues, some of whom may have been candidates for your job. Disappointment can take different people in different ways. Some may be cheerfully philosophical, and be perfectly willing to march behind your banner. Others may be nursing severely damaged egos which cause them to respond negatively whenever new ideas are discussed.

During the first few weeks of your appointment, you can afford to be magnanimous and, aided by your supporters, do your best to win over any boardroom dissidents. Focus your efforts upon whichever individual appears to be their spokesman (rest assured there will always be one!). More often than not, given a judicious blend of firmness and flattery – and not a little patience – the ice will eventually begin to melt and the 'management team' will become a team in reality. But should the individual(s) show no sign of wishing to cooperate, then he/they must be removed. Healthy debate is one thing, organised opposition quite another. You cannot hope to fight the competition successfully, still less to grow the company, if you are constantly on the look-out for potential Brutuses. Strike hard, and get it over with as quickly as possible. Better to lose a few people in the early stages than to face constant intrigues throughout your reign.

Right from the start your most important task is to provide employees with a vision of the company's future which they find credible, attractive, and to which they can commit their energies unreservedly. But before you can carry your message to the people you have first to convince your boardroom colleagues that your Promised Land is both attainable and worth attaining. Your grand strategy, whatever its timescale – five, ten, perhaps even twenty years – must be based upon a realistic appraisal of the resources currently available to you; and what they can be expected to produce. Additional resources must be specified – and justified – and methods of funding them clearly argued. Above all, proposals for new products or services need to be underpinned by thorough market research and, where appropriate, by consumer testing. This is no time for investing in expensive follies which may owe more to human egotism than to the demands of the marketplace.

Ought you to make a point of occasionally attending other key meetings which up till now have not normally been attended by the chief executive? Here again there are powerful arguments for squeezing such meetings into your already crowded schedule, even if you are only able to stay for a relatively short time. Not only will you increase your knowledge of some of the major issues in the various segments of the business, but you will also have an opportunity of assessing the quality of the proposed strategies and the calibre of those discussing them.

Look out for three types of contributor in particular. First, the *mavericks,* those innovative thinkers who refuse to be shackled by tradition: these are the ones who can save you money, win new customers and sharpen the company's competitive edge. Second, watch out for those tough-minded *pragmatists,* who focus upon results and whether an idea can be made to work: they are the ones who make things happen. Finally, try to spot the *bridge-builders,* people who make up in statesmanship what they may lack in charisma. These are those consistently constructive contributors who help to overcome deadlocks, soothe bruised egos and keep the discussion moving forward. They are worth their weight in gold to any chairman.

— *Challenging the culture* —

Anyone who wants to change things – and that, basically, is what chief executives are *for* – must expect to encounter a degree of opposition, for many human beings are apprehensive about change, suspecting that it may threaten their job security or present them with the challenge of learning new skills. Yet frequently your most powerful opponent of all is something which, though invisible, holds sway over men's minds, shaping their attitudes and governing their behaviour. This, of course, is that most potent of tranquillisers, the corporate culture: 'the way we do things around here (so don't rock the boat if you want to be accepted)'.

Now assuming that you have been in the company for at least a few years, you will have a clear understanding of what you are up against. You will already have formed an opinion of those elements in the culture which are valuable and worth preserving and those which, if unchallenged, could prove fatal to your plans. The main ingredients of such a lethal brew might include the current company organisation structure, the refusal to diversify outside a narrow product range or to invest in new technologies and the failure to plan for management succession. Such weaknesses will, of course, be defended and justified by an infinite variety of cracker-barrel philosophies, ranging from 'a company should stick to what it does best' to 'a good man will always get to the top, with or without formal training'. It is not that such concepts are entirely without merit. It is the rigid refusal to consider alternatives.

Confronting corporate tradition head-on is a daunting task, even for a chief executive, but it is a challenge which must be met if you are to make your mark. Yet it is no use attacking simultaneously on all fronts and being easily repulsed; instead, concentrate your fire on a few key objectives where the prospects of a breakthrough are reasonably high. For example, a few modest strategic acquisitions which bring in new products and new technologies will send a clear signal to the organisation that you intend to break the existing product mould. Again, the recruitment of a number of high-calibre executives and key specialists from other companies will show that you are determined to sweep away the cobwebs of parochial thinking. And if you attend one or two high-level seminars yourself, it will come as no surprise when you initiate a number of new approaches to management development.

But it is not only the major strategic changes which can help you to demonstrate that times are a-changing: sometimes even relatively minor changes can send powerful signals about your values and beliefs. For example, a requirement that the senior executive dining room may be used only to entertain important visitors to the company, and that senior executives (including yourself) should otherwise eat in the main staff restaurant will undoubtedly displease those who delight in their elitist privileges. But for every such complainant there will be many, many more employees at all levels who will heave a sigh of relief that at last top management is taking positive steps to improve communication and teamwork. And if you yourself make a point of lunching with different groups of employees whenever you are in the restaurant, your example will be noted by other senior people and, more importantly, followed. It is upon such seemingly trivial actions that your image in the organisation will be based, rather than on reports of your speeches in the company newspaper.

Establishing yourself as the boss of an organisation, be it a giant multinational or a small family business is like appearing at a Royal Command Performance: the opportunities to succeed or fail are about evenly balanced. However, one thing is certain: you will be totally exposed. Your every decision, your every action, dramatic or commonplace, will be critically evaluated and interpreted by people who, for the most part, have no particular interest in, or grasp of, strategic business issues, but are concerned primarily with their own jobs, their own careers, their own security. Yet somehow you must find the time and the means to convince this polyglot army that you are a leader worth following and that, by helping you to achieve your objectives, they can also achieve theirs. It is a formidable task, requiring determination and stamina of the highest order. But as you bring the ship home safely into harbour you may reflect that you would not have it any other way.

Chapter 18

PICKING A WINNING TEAM

Weed out the weaklings – but do it compassionately.

The fact that you have dealt firmly with those members of the Board who clearly had no intention of cooperating and, had they remained unchecked, would have been a thorn in your side, does not in any way imply that you should be seeking to captain a team of sycophants and yes-men. Like any other executive, you are judged by the company you keep and, if you are to generate the kind of loyalty and enthusiasm which encourages employees to give willingly of their best, then you need to surround yourself with able people: people who are prepared to speak their minds and to comment objectively on your strategies and plans. In short, you need executives who will keep you on your toes.

— *Assessing your resources* —

The top management team which you have inherited from your predecessor may not be the one which you need to achieve your objectives. Even after you have got rid of any malcontents, there may well be some weaknesses which demand to be rectified. And since some of these 'low flyers' may be long-serving employees who are popular in the company, such matters may require sensitive handling and, above all, scrupulous fairness.

Each member of your team should be subjected to the same informal, yet highly rigorous, assessment process: your personal feelings towards an individual must not be permitted to cloud your business judgement. As a first step, interview each of your immediate subordinates and get them to talk about their jobs, their achievements and their plans for the future. Don't keep interrupting them or arguing with them: your job is to *listen*. Ask the occasional question only to keep them on track, or to revitalise them if they appear to be running out of steam. Nevertheless, these questions should be *penetrating*; aimed at uncovering not merely facts, but also those motivations and attitudes which govern behaviour.

During each of these interviews, three questions should be uppermost in your mind. First, how *intelligent* is this person: will he or she have the mental firepower to do the kind of job which needs to be done? Second, how *determined* is this individual: can he or she convert ideas into action, overcome setbacks and show drive and persistence in pursuing tough objectives? Third, is this person an *enthusiast* who can generate such enthusiasm in others that they achieve things which they never dreamed they were capable of achieving? In brief, you are looking for evidence of *leadership*, that golden quality which ignites commitment, harnesses effort, unleashes creativity and, most importantly, gets results.

Make sure, too, that you do your homework: thoroughly investigate each individual's track record. If the person concerned has been running a business with full profit responsibility, find out if profits have grown, declined or remained fairly steady, and what the reasons were for these results. Try to assess the impact of the particular market environment in which each individual has been operating. Some may have had a lucky break; for example, government legislation may have created a vast new market for the product. Others may have been battling gamely to sell an overpriced product of inferior quality in an overcrowded market (and, if so, what plans do they have for becoming more competitive or,if the situation seems hopeless, for withdrawing from the market?).

Directors of staff departments should be judged on whether their services to the line groups are perceived by their 'clients' as relevant, helpful, technically sound and capable of responding to changing demands. Any evidence of bureaucratic rigidity and inertia, or of 'sacred cow' policies which appear to be written in stone, should cause you to ponder whether the executive responsible is capable of adapting to an environment in which continuous change is a prerequisite of survival. Indeed, a performance yardstick which may be fairly applied to senior executives in both line and staff groups is whether they have shown a capacity for innovation, or have been content merely to plod along an all too familiar path which can only lead to stagnation and a loss of competitiveness.

Having completed your evaluation of your senior colleagues, you can now divide them into three groups: those who are clearly capable of meeting the challenges which you have in store for them; those who are borderline cases, but have done enough to deserve a second chance, at least for a further six months; and those who are not going to make it and must be replaced. Be warned: it is your treatment of this last group which will determine whether you are perceived as a ruthless hatchet-man or as a vigorous new broom who is merely trying to secure the company's future. The golden rule is to be as generous as possible. Those whom you intend to remove should be offered any other senior or middle-ranking post which would give them an opportunity to use their strengths. If such posts are not available, then their severance terms should fully reflect the company's gratitude for their past contributions.

Recruiting outsiders

While there is nothing wrong with a general policy of 'promotion from within', there is much to be said for the occasional infusion of new blood from outside, particularly into key line jobs where there is a question mark over the calibre of the internal candidates.

But how do you attract the right people and, having done so, select them?

Whether you use headhunters or advertise in the quality press, the first thing to decide upon is the job specification. Here you must try to strike a balance between being so imprecise that virtually any moderately competent executive could apply for the job, and being so exacting that you might just as well demand the ability to walk on water. The rule here, as in all successful communication, is to say what you mean and mean what you say. If you are convinced that a certain paper qualification, say an MBA, is necessary as evidence of the required level of mental acuity, then say so; if not, don't. Then again, if there are certain kinds of experience which you consider crucial (not merely desirable), use them when you carry out your first cull of the replies you receive. But keep such 'exclusion factors' to the minimum. By narrowing the field too soon, you run the risk of missing some excellent people. Track record and personality do not always leap out from application letters and forms.

If you decide to use headhunters to produce a short list, recognise that you are delegating your judgement to someone else, so it is vital to use only skilled professionals. In spite of the mystique which surrounds headhunting, it is by no means a sure-fire method of unearthing the right candidate: indeed, all too often, as with any advisory service, it is merely an easy way of wasting a great deal of money. The remedy is obvious: choose your headhunter as carefully as you would if he or she were the candidate.

Above all, be on your guard against those so-called 'selection consultants', who would have you believe that executive talent can be unerringly pinpointed by a battery of 'tests' whose validity and reliability may be highly suspect. For despite all the pseudo academic flim-flam and sub-Jungian posturing by the more brazen peddlars of these products, the predictive value of such tests is scarcely better than you could achieve by flipping a coin. Why, then, do they continue to flourish? The sad fact is that many senior appointments are made by people who either have little confidence in their own judgement, or are terrified of making an expensive mistake. The dubious test merchants are simply the latest in a long line of witchdoctors and sorcerers who appear to offer an easy way out of the pressures of decision making. The truth is that there is no escape. No test, reputable or otherwise, can know what *you* know about the job. Only *you* can know the right questions to ask. And only *you* can judge whether an individual is likely to fit into your management team. In short, selecting people who will enrich their jobs and grow the company is a job which only you can do. It is an essential part of your executive accountability.

Nonetheless, you will need to be at your sharpest, for at this level of recruitment there is never a lack of sycophants to massage your ego, or of smooth-talking 'strategists' with every apparent virtue except common sense. The only way of sifting the gold from the dross is to dissect each candidate's track record with meticulous care, forever probing motivations, assessing values and standards and, terrier-like, digging deep into the candidate's claimed successes in order to find out whether a particular achievement was truly his or hers or merely the product of a long-established system.

And however careful the initial vetting process may have been, there are bound to be occasions when unsuitable candidates somehow slip through the net. Beware, for example, the loud-voiced extrovert with a grip of steel, who sees himself as a Colossus towering over a rabble of mean-spirited superiors and envious colleagues, none of whom appear to appreciate his supercharged talents; the all-too-glib individual who has left a succession of jobs because of 'policy differences'; and, not least, the bright-eyed young thruster who, scarcely six months since his last promotion, is already seeking a 'new challenge'. Verily, by their evasions ye shall know them.

Forget those boy-scout books on leadership with their utopian visions of philosopher-executives who seem to spend their time churning out mission statements like railway timetables. Look instead for the quiet achievers, ambitious yet realistic, assertive yet modest, proud of their achievements yet not afraid to acknowledge their own human fallibility. These are the ones who will enjoy discussing with you not only what was achieved, but how it was achieved and what they learned from both success and failure. For make no mistake: it is this capacity to learn and to grow which outranks virtually every other executive quality, except for integrity. Charlatans may bluster, and con-men may deceive, but the kind of people you need are driven by the most powerful of all internal demons: a passion for excellence and a thirst for self-respect.

Conducting the interview

The best prediction of what an executive is likely to do in the future is a penetrating study of what he or she has done in the past. The reason why so many interviews are ineffective is that interviewers don't ask the right questions; questions which focus on the candidate's accomplishments rather than on whether he or she has a 'well-balanced personality'. What we should be seeking at senior management level is not well-balanced mediocrities for whom such work is simply a means of achieving a comfortable affluence, but assertive, innovative risk-takers who will build the business as well as their own careers. Things which are perfectly balanced often stand still.

So how can you distinguish the achievers from the talkers? Here are some questions which, if you listen carefully to the answers (and keep on probing until you are satisfied) should help you to decide whether you are talking to the right person:

1. Let's focus on your current job. What are your key objectives this year? How satisfied are you with progress to date?
2. What achievements during the past year are you most proud of, and why?
3. What do you see as the three greatest strengths of your current

operation? Which are the weaker areas and what plans do you have for improving their performance?

4 Tell me about the people who report to you. How do you measure their performance? How do you motivate them? How are you developing them for additional responsibility? Have you developed someone who could take over the job?
5 What departments do you have to work with closely in order to achieve your objectives? What kind of problems come up and how do you overcome them? Are there any unresolved issues which you are currently working on?
6 Give me some examples of significant innovations which you have originated and implemented during the past year. What difficulties did you encounter and how did you deal with them? What have been the benefits to date and what further benefits do you expect in the future?
7 How would you define your personal management style? How do you feel it might be perceived by your subordinates? Of the various bosses you have worked with during your career whose style were you most comfortable with, and why?

You may or may not choose to take notes during the interview, but as soon as it is over, put down your impressions on paper while they are still fresh in your mind. Make a thumb-nail sketch of each candidate under such headings as strengths and weaknesses, biases and preferences, blind spots and quirks, and personal acceptability and interpersonal skills. Mull over the pros and cons of each contender for a day or two, but don't take too long. After all, there is only one question that really matters: who would I want on the bridge with me when the going gets rough? If there is no one who appeals to you, tear up the shortlist and start again. There is too much at stake to risk settling for second-best.

Finally, examine your own performance. Were you overly influenced by first impressions and spent most of the interview trying to confirm them? Did you or the candidates do the bulk of the talking? Was the atmosphere relaxed but businesslike? In short, did you do a *professional* job?

Introducing new talent

Let us assume that you have selected your new executives and that they are about to join you. How can you ensure that they adapt as quickly as possible to what may well be a very different environment from the one they have just left?

There are three key areas which must be covered during the settling-in process: company strategies, company politics, and your own expectations regarding each individual's performance. Company strategies must not, of course, be discussed in isolation, but in terms of how they fit into your vision of the future: the kind of organisation you dream of creating. Make it clear to your new lieutenants that, though the vision itself is not negotiable, the contributing strategies most certainly are. Tell them that you will be looking for – indeed encouraging – the sort of well-researched constructive criticism which can only speed the accomplishment of your vision, and that there are no sacred cows or forbidden topics.

Company politics is a more delicate area, and one which requires a sensitive touch. Basically, you need to brief the newcomers on the motivating traditions and values of the organisation, including the key 'people philosophies', the way in which power and influence are distributed at the top echelons, how policy decisions are arrived at and communicated, and how you expect any differences with colleagues to be resolved. Make it plain that you are not seeking the kind of bland atmosphere, so typical of many large organisations, in which executives engage in polite ritual dances with each other, while resentments and frustrations simmer just below the surface. There will be no 'black marks' for those who speak their minds, only for those who personalise differences and allow them to sour their enthusiasm.

Spell out your performance expectations to each individual loud and clear; not simply the specific goals you want accomplished, but the manner of their accomplishment: the spirit and sheer verve which you expect to see employed. Make it clear that the ability to manage change and to build and sustain enthusiasm are the two key competencies which you will be looking for, not short-term gimmicks which might give a quick boost to profits, but could damage future growth. In short, don't be afraid to disclose your own values, for without such frankness – which must be mutual – it can be difficult to build a trusting relationship.

Of all the challenges facing a newly-appointed top executive, picking a winning team is one of the most difficult and rewarding. Leader, motivator, counsellor, critic: these are the essential roles that you must play, each of which demands complex social skills. Yet there is no escape from that ultimate imperative of every effective leader: to create something which is greater than the sum of its parts. Whether it is your own performance or that of others, *this* must be the yardstick. You cannot ask for more, nor should you settle for less.

Chapter 19

LIVING WITH STRESS

Positive thinking is the only way to beat it.

You would not have reached your present position if you had not revelled in the challenge of coping with stress. Unlike many of your competitors who fell by the wayside, you had the psychological toughness to roll with the punches, to shrug off setbacks, and to remain calm and purposeful. Panics and crises, disappointments and let-downs were no more to you than passing mosquito bites: irritating perhaps, but scarcely lethal. Pressure was simply another word for opportunity. The only thing you dreaded was a problem-free life.

Nevertheless, now that you are running the company, you need a positive strategy for dealing with stress, since you are bound to encounter powerful new pressures, many of which are unique to your position. You are now fully accountable for the performance of the entire organisation: for its profits and losses, its acquisitions and divestments, its corporate image in the wider community, its morale and the quality of the people who work for it. No longer can you point an accusing finger at some higher executive. You alone are flying the plane.

It follows as surely as night follows day that you need a strategy for coping with your *total life*, not simply that part of it which you spend at work. For most human beings, work and leisure are not separate compartments, but merely different arenas in which they display their qualities. And as a chief executive who is forever 'on show', your prime requirement is to achieve a balance between your personal life and the demands of the job.

— *Get your relationships right* —

Some chief executives surround themselves with flatterers and sycophants who can be relied upon to endorse their every action, thus avoiding the wear-and-tear of honest debate. Small wonder that they lose their cutting edge (and, even more disastrously, their grip upon reality), for it is the flint against the rock which produces the spark. Make sure that the people who report to you are bright enough and confident enough to tell you when you are about to make a fool of yourself. They can hardly render you a more valuable service.

This means that they must have room to breathe and freedom to manoeuvre; in other words, that they must be entrusted with a degree of autonomy which befits their talents. True, no one should doubt who is in charge on the bridge, but you need people beside you who will use their initiative to help you keep the ship on course. Encourage your captains to act like captains, and to thoroughly critique even your most cherished plans. If frankness is the tribute that one owes to one's friends, then do everything you can to win their friendship.

It won't be easy. Remember, you carry a great deal of firepower, and even confident, high-calibre people sometimes hesitate to level with the Top Man (or Woman) upon whom they rely for their authority and status, and who one day they may hope to succeed. The only way that you can win their friendship is to act like a friend, and do those things that good friends do. This means not merely throwing the occasional dinner party, or arranging, rather more frequently, a round of golf. It means being bold enough to exchange confidences, and to say what you really think (except, of course, about your colleague's peers). Mutual trust is a two-way street, and it is up to you to take the first step.

By establishing frank and open relationships with the people who report to you, you can not only enhance their commitment and motivation, you can also remove a primary source of self-inflicted stress. All too many chief executives keep their subordinates at arm's length, and then worry about whether they are pulling their weight or plotting against them. Open relationships are far less stressful. To win confidence, you must first confide.

— *Be a good listener* —

A great deal of stress results from poor communication, from people not knowing what is 'going on'. And since the top of the mountain is a long way from the plain below, it is all too easy for a chief executive to get out of touch and to live in a world where there is only good news, any bad news being concealed until the last possible moment. The impact of the bad news, when it finally arrives, is like a sudden storm on a hitherto sunny day, and can be devastatingly stressful for those involved. It is at times like these that coronaries strike, and many seek relief in alcohol and tranquillisers.

If you want to avoid this kind of stress, practise the skills of effective listening, and make communicating with you a rewarding experience. By keeping interruptions to an absolute minimum, and by maintaining an alert and attentive posture, you can earn a reputation as being 'someone you can talk to'. Not only will this do wonders for your image in the company, it will encourage your colleagues to communicate frankly and honestly. No longer will they shrink from discussing their problems for fear of running a gauntlet of tetchy interruptions, frequently based upon ignorance of the facts. Confident that they will receive a fair hearing, the data that they give you is likely to be both accurate and complete.

But there is a subtler point which makes effective listening not simply good business, but good leadership behaviour. Respect for a person's human dignity is a key component of any leadership strategy which seeks to generate self-motivation and willing cooperation. By listening to someone who is trying to communicate with you, you are signalling that you respect the speaker *as a person*; that you recognise his or her knowledge, skill and experience. People who receive respect from others tend to give it to others. Such relationships are invariably far less stressful than those which are based upon intolerance and fear.

— *Cut down on meetings* —

When the top person in an organisation becomes stressed, the effect can be progressively destructive throughout the whole management team. Deadlines are missed, business is lost, relationships suffer and a feeling of malaise hovers over the executive suite. It is no use just hoping that the situation will correct itself – it won't. What is required is not fatalism, but swift and purposeful action from the organisation's chief example-setter. You.

Concentrate first on identifying the chief stressors in your working life. For example, do you find yourself attending too many meetings both inside and outside the company? Do such meetings result in your working excessively long hours or in your having to take work home at weekends? It is not heroic but foolish to endure a working lifestyle which reduces your value to the organisation which employs you. So put every meeting which you attend on trial for its life. Ask yourself whether your attendance is essential or merely traditional. If the latter, then either pull out of such meetings, or cancel them altogether. As for those meetings which you continue to hold, be a touch more demanding in the way you run them. Set a time by which you expect the meeting to have finished, discourage verbose or irrelevant contributions, and show that you have 'done your homework', i.e. that you have read all the documentation relating to the agenda, and that you expect others to have done the same.

Travelling to distant locations can also be a major source of stress for many chief executives, particularly when it involves major changes of climate. Admittedly, much of this type of travelling is inevitable in order to keep in touch with important customers and suppliers, to seek out new business, and to evaluate the performance of overseas management. But here again modern communications technology presents chief executives with many opportunities to reduce the stress involved in continual travelling. For example, some organisations with many small locations in third-world countries send regular video cassettes to their overseas subsidiaries, featuring the chief executive and other members of the top management team. Typical subjects covered include business results, plans for the future, imminent changes in policies and procedures, and congratulatory messages to particular companies or individuals for outstanding performance. There is, of course, no real substitute for the personal touch, but if such methods can result in a significant reduction in this kind of travel-induced stress, both individuals and organisations can only benefit.

Much the same effect can be achieved by the use of tele-conferencing, a technique whereby individuals in a number of locations can be linked by CCTV, and can thus participate in a meeting without leaving their offices. While differences in time zones can sometimes make such meetings difficult to organise, the highly participative nature of the method gives it a significant advantage over video recordings.

— *Delegate* —

If you want to condemn yourself to the prospect of an early coronary, then go ahead: try to do everything yourself. Truly, there is no greater disservice that you can perform for yourself, your organisation and those who work for you. No conductor is expected to play every instrument in the orchestra better than the musicians who play them, and no chief executive is expected to know or do everything. Set challenging goals, identify the data you need to measure performance, and then give your people the freedom to perform. Your regular progress reviews will tell you whether you need to intervene.

There is no more potent stress-reliever than a vigorous policy of *planned delegation*. It means examining your job and asking yourself three searching questions:

1 Why do *I* do this task?
2 Which of my subordinates could do it for me *now*?
3 Who could do it *after some further coaching or training*?

Delegation is the oxygen of any healthy enterprise. It means that, throughout the organisation, people are being provided with opportunities to go on growing and developing their abilities. It means that they are being challenged to learn new skills. And, not least, it means that they are being protected against that most insidious of demotivators: boredom. When boredom takes over, stagnation can never be far behind, and stagnation and stress are like Siamese twins.

As for yourself, the main benefit is that you will have more time for those things which lie at the heart of the chief executive's role: strategic planning, coordination and, above all, leadership. Positioned as you are at the pinnacle of the company, no one is better placed to generate those feelings of optimism and self-confidence which make everyone feel part of a winning team.

Relaxez-vous

Whatever you choose to do in your leisure time ought to relax you, not stress you: this is the main drawback with such highly competitive games as squash and golf, both of which have as great a capacity to increase tension as to reduce it. As regards active pursuits, walking is generally the most relaxing, particularly if it can be combined with some specialist interest such as birdwatching.

The guiding principle should be to distance yourself as far as possible from your life-style at work, and to tune in to an entirely different set of pursuits and, if possible, a different environment. A cottage in a part of the countryside which particularly appeals to you, a weekend break in a country hotel, a flying visit to, say, Paris or Madrid: these are but some of the myriad ways in which you can 'get away from it all', if only for a few days. Whether you enjoy fishing for trout or observing wildlife in some rain-soaked hide, one thing is certain: you will recharge your batteries and come back refreshed.

Don't spoil your leisure hours by burying yourself in those financial newspapers and business magazines which you read every day on your way to the office. Choose a book or magazine connected with one of your interests or hobbies or, if you feel the need for something more intellectually stimulating, read a biography of some great historical figure whom you have always admired. Tastes in literature, of course, can differ profoundly between individuals but many chief executives have found authors like Trollope, Hardy and Graham Greene particularly rewarding with their penetrating studies of human motivation. But in the final analysis, it's up to you. Read whatever you find most relaxing and personally rewarding.

Feel good about yourself

People who attain pole positions in organisations are not generally lacking in either self-confidence or self-esteem: they could hardly have travelled so far without believing in themselves. Nevertheless, behind that extrovert personality and forceful manner, there sometimes lies a surprisingly fragile ego which is by no means as disaster-proof as appearances might suggest. And even the most balanced and self-confident high achievers occasionally find themselves having 'a bad patch' when nothing seems to go right. It is at times like these that you need a kind of psychological first-aid kit to ward off depression and negative thinking.

There is no mystery involved here, no exotic mantras or deep-breathing exercises. Simply take a sheet of paper and write down a list of accomplishments which you regard as the highlights of your business career, especially those which relate to your current job. Alternatively, you could list the knowledge and skills, social as well as technical, which have helped to propel you to your present heights. Make no mistake: this is *not* an exercise in self-congratulation or an attempt to gloss over those areas of your performance where you know you need to improve. It is simply an exercise in *positive thinking*: a perfectly legitimate listing of your achievements and skills which has the effect of encouraging you to deal confidently with your current problems. It also helps you to keep a sense of proportion about these problems which, in some instances, may be no more challenging than many others which you have solved in the past.

As an extension of the same confidence-boosting approach, you could also list those achievements *outside* your working life which have given you the greatest satisfaction. These could include such areas as your marriage, your children, your home, your work for charity, even the pleasure of having created a beautiful garden. The point is that just as you take steps to safeguard your physical health as a matter of course, so you must be equally assiduous in performing those mental exercises, which will increase your confidence in your ability to deal with your problems. Both mind and body need to be kept in trim.

Finally, there are times when the best – indeed the only – defence against stress is, in effect, to laugh in the face of adversity, since there will be moments when you can do no more, and when your fate rests simply upon a turn of life's wheel. And just as you need to develop a success philosophy which enables you to scale the commanding heights, so too you need a mind-set, which will help you to ride those fearsome downwaves which can threaten to engulf even the most promising career. If you are confident that you have done all you can to deal with a problem, then sit tight and hope for the best. What will be will be, and to go on worrying is to hurt no one but yourself.

Chapter 20

STAYING ON TOP

Keep on learning – an obsolescent chief executive lives on borrowed time.

The fact that you are the chief executive in no way enhances your job security: quite the opposite. Total accountability equals total vulnerability, and the pressure to perform increases, not diminishes, when you reach the top. No one else in the organisation has to make the same critical (and sometimes lethal) choices between long-term strategy and short-term profit, between survival tomorrow and success today. And should things go wrong, there are always plenty of believers in human sacrifice as the only way to change a company's luck. Investors' 'lack of confidence in the management team', especially on the part of institutional fund managers, has led to the downfall of many a superstar who only yesterday had seemed impregnable.

Make no mistake: the only way you can secure your position is to achieve or, better still, surpass the results which are expected of you. This means that in order to survive you must go on growing as an executive; that you must leave yourself open to new knowledge, new skills, new ideas, new experiences. Slam the door on new thinking, institutionalise your prejudices, worship the same old sacred cows, and the ice beneath your feet will grow thinner every day. It is not a question of living dangerously, for as the company's chief risk-taker you have little choice. It is more a question of taking the right risks, of eschewing soft options and, above all, of setting the right example.

Don't be afraid to trust your intuition sometimes. If you have learned to analyse your successes and failures, you can face the future with plenty of confidence.

— Test the organisation —

'Keep close to the customer' has long been the battle-cry of a multitude of organisations but all too often it has remained a mere incantation, a toothless tiger which can scarcely raise a roar. 'Customer care' means more, much more, than improving quality control procedures, or running 'quality colleges' for supervisors and middle management. It means continually putting yourself in the place of the customer, seeing what he sees and hearing what he hears. It means getting out of your office and actually visiting a whole range of customers and finding out how *they* see the product or service, and in what ways *they* feel improvements could be made. Above all, it means listening and learning, not making excuses or becoming defensive.

A programme of customer visits, swiftly followed by meetings with the appropriate executives in your own organisation, will do more to spread the gospel of 'the customer comes first' than any amount of exhortation or formal indoctrination. People at any level in an organisation are far more impressed by what the boss does, rather than by what he or she says. And they will be even more impressed when they find out that you have been following up with some of the customers you have visited to check that the quality of the service has improved. Those cynics who sneered that it was just another gimmick will have been put to flight. It will be clear beyond doubt that you mean what you say.

Finally, there is much to be said for occasionally doing a job which brings you into direct contact with customers, or at least enables you to observe how they are being treated. A day spent manning the reception desk in an hotel or service station, a few days in a sales office dealing with customer enquiries, a spell on the road with a service engineer: these are just a few of the many ways in which you can find out what is really happening. Don't be put off by those who grumble that such work is a waste of your very expensive time: it isn't. There is no more important task in any organisation than satisfying the customer. If you want the message to have impact then get involved yourself.

— *Keep the ideas coming* —

Keep specialist staff groups to the minimum, and get rid of them wherever possible. Quality, for example, is everyone's responsibility: having a specialist department signals just the opposite. Nor should you allow human resources groups to become so densely populated that line management begins to abdicate its people responsibilities. True, you may need a few professional advisers, but resist any attempts to persuade you that you need a ponderous 'infrastructure'. Line managers must learn how to handle their people problems, and prove themselves capable of recruiting, selecting and training their staff. Those who say they have no time for such tasks are saying, in effect, that they have no interest in managing. They should be reminded where their priorities should lie, that people are their most precious resource.

Promote people with good ideas, and give them sufficient resources to put their theories into practice. If the organisation has a management appraisal scheme, make sure that criteria such as 'creativity' or 'innovation' are prominently featured in the list of performance factors. Run competitions and award worthwhile prizes to both groups and individuals who come up with new and creative solutions to problems, especially those which have a direct impact upon customer relations. Encourage even the most junior levels of employees, white or blue collar, to keep their eyes and ears open, and to come forward with suggestions for improvements. Get rid of any supervisors or managers who consistently try to block new ideas, and replace them with people with more commitment. Make certain that the names and photographs of your prize-winning innovators appear on the appropriate notice boards and in the company newspaper. In short, generate an 'ideas culture' which is open to everyone and from which everyone can benefit.

Don't expect miracles overnight. In some cases you will be dealing with people who for many years may have been actively discouraged from thinking for themselves and are, not surprisingly, lacking in self-confidence. This makes it all the more imperative for you to get personally involved in recognising their efforts. Don't delegate your role at the awards ceremony to someone else: handle it yourself. Most people enjoy having their contributions recognised and there's no more gratifying form of personal recognition than praise from the chief executive, no matter what other 'motivators' are being used.

Keep a high profile

It's just as vital to keep your employees motivated as it is to keep your customers happy for poor morale soon affects both quality and service. Maintaining the enthusiasm of your managers and workforce is partly a question of managing the working environment but, much more importantly, of winning their hearts and minds.

It goes without saying that the company's wages, salaries and benefits should be competitive for the industry, that they should be regularly reviewed, and that jobs should be graded by reference to yardsticks which are seen (at least by the great majority of employees) as relevant and objective. Your main responsibility in this highly emotive area of tangible rewards is to ensure that your systems are being managed by professionals, and that they are technically sound and politically defensible. Money may not be everything, but despite the rather dismissive comments of some behavioural scientists it remains for most people a very clear indicator of their value to the company.

As regards the actual working environment, the key goal for any chief executive who is really serious about improving teamwork must be to reduce and, as soon as possible, abolish those irritating bits of 'petty apartheid' which do so much to perpetuate a 'them and us' atmosphere in so many organisations. There really is no justification for making 'staff restaurants' and 'works canteens' into mutually exclusive 'no go areas', for separate car parks and reserved parking spaces, for separate lavatories and recreational facilities, for 'executive dining rooms' reserved exclusively for directors. While abolishing such divisive traditions may be a long-term project, it is never too early to make a start. After all, who ever heard of a successful modern cricket captain treating some of his team as 'gentlemen' and the rest as 'players'? Double standards and team spirit just do not mix.

But unquestionably the area in which you can make your most powerful contribution to employee morale is exactly where you would expect it to be: in providing highly visible personal leadership. It is hard for troops to have much faith in a general who they never see, and so the occasional visit to even your most distant outposts will be greatly appreciated by employees, who may sometimes feel that they have been forgotten. The surprise visit to a head office department with many junior staff, or an unscheduled appearance on the shop floor can also result in much favourable comment, especially if you chat to as many people as possible and show a genuine interest in their work. Ignore those who tell you that 'all they're interested in is money'. Such comments tell you more about the leadership problems of the speaker than about the people you will be meeting.

Take the initiative in communicating. Don't allow rumours to sweep through the organisation like a bush fire; call as many meetings as are necessary to put employees' minds at rest. Remember that, for the vast majority of people, job security is the keystone of their lives, and anything which may threaten it is bound to worry them. Fear of the possible consequences of takeovers and mergers, the loss of important customers and rumours of redundancies, adverse comments in the financial press: these are just a few of the many worrying scenarios which can cause morale to plummet. Once again, setting the record straight is a task which you must handle yourself, for no one else has your authority and credibility. What you have to tell them may not always be palatable, but at least you will earn respect for being a 'straight shooter'. And establishing mutual trust is what leadership is all about.

Insist that all managers follow your example and communicate with their people. Reward those who do and replace those who don't. Clearly they shouldn't be leading a team.

— *Establishing the core values* —

Remember: a whisper from the top can sound like a thunderclap two levels below. As chief executive, your decisions and actions will be scrutinised and judged, not simply for their professional 'soundness', but for what they may reveal about your own values and standards. Your official statements on myriad subjects, your policy decisions, your expressions of approval and disapproval, even your throwaway comments on social occasions: all will be eagerly examined for evidence of the kind of person that you really are. The reason for this interest is that people like to be led by a flesh-and-blood person to whom they can relate, not by a remote deity whom they rarely see.

In every organisation, anecdotes abound of how the chief executive acted or reacted in a particular situation, business or social, so that people gradually begin to feel that they know the 'big boss' and can predict how he or she will behave. While there is no way in which you can hope to eliminate such highly-coloured gossip, you can at least try to ensure that it runs in your favour. To do this you need to display two key qualities: courage and consistency. For example, you will be perceived as *courageous* if you are seen to be standing up to ill-founded attacks upon the company, say from the media, which could damage its reputation and threaten jobs. You will be perceived as *consistent* when you are seen to be applying the same rigorous standards to your own subordinates as you exhort others to apply to theirs. Whether it be a shortfall in performance or a lapse in personal behaviour, the way that you deal with the offender will be critically examined for signs of inconsistency, especially those dreaded 'double standards' which, once detected, can do so much to undermine a leader's credibility.

The truth is that you occupy the one position in the organisation where you can never avoid the spotlight's glare. But you can turn this to your advantage by seizing every possible opportunity to hammer home those 'core values' which you see as critical to the company's success, and which you are determined should take root: product quality and concern for the customer; innovation, creativity and zestful performance; teamwork and esprit de corps; integrity and an open management style. Whether you are chatting to individuals or addressing large groups, these are the themes to which you must return over and over again, for without constant reinforcement standards may slip, and a gap open up between theory and practice. The price of excellence is eternal vigilance.

Develop yourself – and others

Running a total business is in itself the most effective kind of management education, and certainly the most dynamic. Like any other skill, management requires practice, followed by analysis of performance, followed by still more practice: it is a never-ending cycle of doing and reflecting. Nevertheless, there will be times when you will need to stand back from all that thrusting and parrying and lay yourself open to new ideas.

There are several ways of doing this. For example, you could enrol for some of those short 'directors' seminars' which are now to be found at most good business schools and management colleges. Here you will be exposed to some of the 'state of the art' thinking in various key management functions, not all of which will be immediately applicable to your current problems, but which will certainly alert you to the shape of things to come.

Equally important, you will have the opportunity to exchange ideas and experiences with people of similar calibre and with similar responsibilities. Whether it be during classroom discussions or over a drink at the bar, you can only benefit by having your ideas and practices challenged by other good minds. If you end up with a deeper appreciation of a number of key issues, and are equipped with a wider range of strategies to deal with them, then the investment of your time will not have been wasted. Indeed it may well have saved you from becoming complacent.

Like any professional group, management teachers vary considerably in their ability to communicate their expertise, and to apply it to the client's practical problems. Nor is it solely a question of professional knowledge and skill: personal compatibility can be just as important. Having found an academic or consultant whom you respect and can get along with, there is much to be said for retaining him or her as a trusted adviser upon whom you can rely for constructive criticism. And since no adviser, however gifted, can be an expert in everything, you may find yourself recruiting others, so that eventually you find yourself presiding over a small, but high-powered 'think tank', dedicated to helping you to generate ideas and, equally important, to making them work.

There is no reason, too, why you should not start your own 'top executive luncheon club'. Once again, either during a management seminar or at some social occasion, you may have identified a few senior businessmen with whom you feel it would be useful to meet to discuss current problems and exchange ideas. While such discussions might occasionally be constrained by the need to maintain tight security on forthcoming strategies and plans, there would still be plenty of opportunities for everyone to benefit. After all, the single richest source of material for management academics is the experience of practical businessmen (often immortalised in voluminous 'case studies'). If businessmen are willing to help academics, why should they shrink from helping themselves?

Finally, while building up your team of external advisers, make sure that you develop your own subordinates. They, too, can benefit from the occasional external course or conference, especially if you brief them carefully before they attend, and discuss what they have learned after they return. A business can only grow if the people who drive it continue to grow, and are constantly stimulated by the challenge of change. So make it clear to your people that they are expected to produce new ideas, to defend them in debate with you and their colleagues and, if they win your approval, to implement them successfully with minimum fuss. Once you can establish the concept that there are no sacred cows, no taboo topics, management teamwork will become a reality. 'Protecting one's turf' will become a thing of the past.

Staying in command of a significant business demands a willingness to be your own toughest critic and the courage to venture into unknown territories where the rewards can be great, but so can the risks. What drives you forward is not so much the prospect of material reward as the compulsion to lead an interesting life where you can use your talents and help others to use theirs. Make no mistake: every successful top executive is a builder, a builder of companies and a builder of people. If you lose that urge then it is time to go, however great the monument you leave behind you.